TRI
AGAIN

TRI
AGAIN

The Road from a
Hospital Bed to Ironman

C H R I S   S H E A R D

First published by Pitch Publishing, 2024

Pitch Publishing
9 Donnington Park,
85 Birdham Road,
Chichester,
West Sussex,
PO20 7AJ
www.pitchpublishing.co.uk
info@pitchpublishing.co.uk

© 2024, Chris Sheard

A CIP catalogue record is available for this book
from the British Library.

ISBN 978 1 80150 913 8

Typesetting and origination by Pitch Publishing

Printed and bound in India by Thomson Press

Contents

'If you want to go fast, go alone.

If you want to go far, go together.'

Part 1: Recovery and Reset

Chapter 1
The Awakening

It's a universally acknowledged truth that no one ever wants to wake up in Trafford Hospital; it's simply not the done thing. Especially not when the sky over Manchester is weeping as if to mourn your dashed Ironman UK dreams. As I lay there, listening to the rain patter against the window, the doctor delivered his prognosis with an air of finality.

'You're certainly not going to be swimming, cycling or running anywhere in the near future, except perhaps in your dreams,' he quipped, a twinkle in his eye that seemed wildly inappropriate given the gravity of my athletic heartbreak.

I stared at him, my response a flat line. 'Most likely caught from open-water swimming, probably something in the water,' he continued, almost smugly. The irony wasn't lost on me; all those mornings I'd cursed the rain as I trained, and now here it was, keeping vigil by my hospital bedside.

Bacterial pneumonia – two words that had swiftly become the bane of my existence, usurping 'interval training' and 'energy gel'. The doctor was chalking it up to bad luck, but I knew the grim truth. My body had been waving a white flag while I pushed it into the red zone, and now here we were.

I tuned back in to the doctor's voice, just as he was saying, '... and with a bit of rest and medication, you should be right as rain in six months or so. Well, maybe not rain, given the circumstances.' He chuckled at his own joke, but I couldn't muster the strength to give him even a pity smile.

The rest of the day was a blur of monotonous hospital routines, punctuated by the unceasing Manchester drizzle that seemed to whisper 'get well soon' in the least convincing manner possible. I was stuck in a bed in Trafford, Manchester, the very heart of the North, where people are known for their resilience. Yet, all I could think about was how my overzealous training had brought me to this point.

Hours turned into days, and the hospital became the centre of my little universe. I was the man who was training for an Ironman but had been taken by something not even visible to the naked eye. My hospital ward bay, with its sterile smell and the constant hum and beeping of machinery, was my new training ground, though the most exercise I got was pressing the nurse call button and shuffling down the hall to a vending machine (drip in hand).

It wasn't just my lungs that needed recovery, it was my pride too. Everyone had known about the Ironman. Work colleagues, family, friends. It was supposed to be my crowning glory, not this. The thought of telling them all about this ignominious setback sat in my stomach like lead.

But as the rain continued to fall outside, I began to find humour in the irony of it all. Yes, I was the man who'd aimed to conquer Ironman UK, only to be conquered by a lake. There was a tragicomic element to it, something almost Shakespearean, if the Bard had been into triathlons and modern medicine.

My wife Briony's visits were the highlight of my day. Her laughter, genuine and warm, filled the room, pushing away the sterile chill. 'So, Ironman, huh?' she'd tease, and I could see the glint of mischief in her eyes. 'You just had to outdo the Manchester weather for drama.'

I grunted in response, feigning annoyance. But the truth was, her banter was a balm to my bruised ego. Would she ever let me live this down? Would she ever let me train for something like this again? She'd allowed me a free pass with the Ironman, letting me spend a small fortune to sign up, and miss even the seemingly most important of family and friends' engagements, flying solo as I went on yet another long cycle ride.

The days in the ward gave me time to think. I mulled over my life choices, the paths I'd taken, and the literal and metaphorical stumbles along the way. My ambition had been a double-edged sword, and I'd managed to nick myself quite spectacularly.

Yet, as I watched the rain streak down the window, I realised that I was undecided about attempting another Ironman. Had the passion for the sport been washed away with the autumn showers, or was it merely put on pause? I wasn't sure, but for now the immediate goals were going to be much smaller, more tangible – to breathe deeply without a wince, to walk the length of the ward without needing a sit-down, and to be allowed back home would be a fine start.

* * *

The rain had become my constant companion, drumming a relentless rhythm against the window pane. It provided a dreary soundtrack to the soap opera of hospital life playing out before me. The characters? A rotating cast of nurses who manoeuvred the blood pressure cuff with the finesse of a Formula 1 pit crew and fellow patients whose snores provided a bizarre bass line to the rhythmic sounds of the machines and hospital dramas.

I had become an unintentional eavesdropper to the soap opera of ward life. By and large the characters on a respiratory ward are not great bedfellows. The hacking, the beeping machines 24/7. Young and old came by. From the curtain-shrouded confessions of a young patient blaming his breathing difficulties on a car accident while sneaking in suspiciously smelling cigarettes, to the brave old men hooked up to so many machines the beeping was reminiscent of a pub gambling machine. It gave some perspective to the hopefully short-term situation I had found myself in.

'Try not to think of it as a setback,' Briony would say, her voice a soothing calm against the antiseptic chill of the room. 'Think of it as an … extended rest period.' Her optimism was admirable, but the only thing 'extended' I was experiencing was the wait for the bathroom.

Each day, the nurses would arrive to take more bloods, the doctor would arrive with his clipboard like a bearer of news from the front. 'Making progress,' he'd announce with a nod that seemed to be more for his benefit than mine. Progress felt like a relative term when the highlight of my day was graduating from soup to solid food.

The irony of my situation was almost laughable. Here I was, a man who had weeks before cycled for so long I'd forgotten what a comfortable seat felt like, now considering the shuffle to the bathroom as the day's main event. My Ironman aspirations had been reduced to this: a man waging a battle of wits against the adjustable bed control.

As the antibiotics did their work, I had time to think, and thinking was a dangerous pastime when your body was idle. The thought of diving back into Ironman training was as daunting as the thought of that first post-hospital run. Would my body cooperate or rebel against me like a teenager asked to clean their room?

The incessant rain mirrored my thoughts – cyclical, persistent and slightly annoying. Briony's visits were the only sunshine, her humour the umbrella under which I found refuge. 'At least you're not having to swim today through this weather,' she'd jest, pointing at the downpour that showed no sign of abating.

With Briony sitting beside me, I found the silver lining. I didn't have to decide my entire future while still within the confines of Trafford Hospital. There was no race signup deadline hanging over my head, no training session I was missing. For the first time in a long while I was on a break, albeit a forced one.

And as I lay there I realised that recovery itself was my new training regimen. Breathing exercises replaced hill sprints, walks down the corridor took the place of endurance cycles, and every spoonful of a hospital dessert was a lesson in overcoming adversity – a taste challenge, if you will.

The week of my hospital stay trudged on, as I began marking time not in hours and minutes but in meals and medication rounds. Each day I felt a little stronger, a little more like myself and a little less like a deflated pool float.

By the time the doctor declared me fit for discharge, the weather had recovered much better than I had. With Briony at my side, we stepped outside and I took a deep breath. The air was fresh, filled with the earthy scent that follows a storm.

'Home time,' Briony said, a smile in her voice. 'And no, we're not discussing any training schedules on the way back.'

I agreed. For now the only schedule I needed was one that included rest, a bit of telly and maybe, just maybe, the contemplation of what lay ahead. Ironman UK had slipped through my fingers, but the journey it had sparked within me was far from over.

As we drove away from Trafford Hospital, the rear-view mirror framed my past week: a chapter closed. But ahead, the road was open, unwritten and brimming with possibility.

And somewhere in the distance I could almost make out the start line of a different kind of race. One that didn't require a wetsuit or a bike, but perhaps something a little more intangible – courage, resilience and a good dose of Mancunian spirit.

Chapter 2
The Collapse

Going back a year prior, and things had been looking significantly rosier. The taste of victory after my first marathon was so sweet, it lingered on my tongue long after the cheers had faded. It seemed to whisper of greater things, of bigger finish lines and personal glory. I had said that the Manchester Marathon would be a one-time-only thing; never again would I put my body through such extreme training. I had aimed to run under four hours, a respectable enough time, and then retire those running shoes forever.

Ah, the Manchester Marathon of 2019, an epic foray into the world of pain, pavement-pounding and public sweating. The route was as diverse as a buffet at a wedding where the bride is from Lancashire and the groom from New Delhi. Starting outside the iconic Old Trafford, the home of Manchester United where dreams and chants soar, the course snaked through the suburban veins of Trafford, Sale and Timperley – each step a further venture into the unknown.

Altrincham greeted us with the kind of cheer usually reserved for victorious gladiators or the end of a particularly long sermon. The air was thick with encouragement and the scent of Deep Heat. We looped back towards Urmston, where legions of supporters lined the streets, their clapping hands and homemade signs a testament to Mancunian solidarity.

As we pounded the storied streets of Stretford, I realised that running a marathon was less about the physical feat and more about a communal trek through the human psyche. There were moments of camaraderie with fellow runners, brief chats that were half pep-talk, half delirium, and all heart.

The miles accumulated like the unread emails in my inbox, but with each new marker the incredulous thought began to simmer – 'I might actually finish this thing, and maybe a little faster than I thought.' And as I passed the invisible baton to my future self at each mile, the endorphins started to whisper sweet nothings about possible victory.

Stretford's stretch was the final act, the crescendo of this pavement opera, and as I neared the finish line, time seemed to slow down – either that or my watch had given up in despair. The supporting crowd's cheering roar was a crescendo, a symphony of support that propelled me forward, their energy infusing my weary legs with a final burst of speed.

Crossing that finish line, the clock stopped at 3 hours 46 minutes. Surprise and delight were understatements. I had done it, run a marathon in a time that wasn't the stuff of legends, but was good enough for me – or at least good enough for a particularly boastful pub story.

The Manchester Marathon had been a journey of self-discovery, a tour of Trafford's finest suburban landscapes, and a testament to what could be achieved with a pair of trainers and a slightly questionable sense of judgment. It was a dance with discomfort, and I had led the tango with surprising agility. And that was me done with marathons, right?

Over the next few months, the itch began to kick in. With my initial goal achieved I let my imagination run away. I devoured books like *Operation Ironman* by George Mahood and *Can't Swim, Can't Bike, Can't Run* by Andy Holgate. Both are tales of everyday people who rose to the challenge of Ironman, and in those pages I found my next challenge. Ironman was no longer a distant dream: it was the next box to tick, the next mountain to climb. If they could do it, surely I could too?

As I enthusiastically shared my decision with Briony over her customary hot chocolate, her reaction was a mixture of pride and practicality. 'You do know what you're signing up for, right?' she questioned, but I was already lost in visions of crossing that epic finish line.

Training kicked off with a passion that bordered on obsession. I pedalled through countryside routes until they blurred into one continuous loop, swam until the pool felt like my second home and ran until my legs pleaded for mercy. But therein lay the flaw to my plan. Without a rigid training regime, I was determined to 'hack' my way to victory. Sign up for a 100-mile bike race around Manchester? I'm in. Swim 2.4 miles every weekend just so I know I can do it? Why not? Try to run a personal best on every run? Let's go for it.

But something insidious was brewing beneath the surface. My cough, initially dismissed as a trivial annoyance, grew persistent, hacking away at my resolve and strength with each passing day. As I should have been peaking, the cough was lingering. But that wasn't all. My energy was seeping away faster than enthusiasm at a snail racing championship, and I was sweating like I'd just run a marathon in a sauna. It was as if my body had decided to throw its own little rebellion party, and every symptom was invited.

At work, it became impossible to hide. My once sporadic cough had evolved into a cacophony that echoed off the office walls, disrupting the daily hum of productivity. My boss, never one to mince words, finally laid down the ultimatum with a sternness I hadn't anticipated. 'You're a wreck,' he said plainly. 'Get to the hospital, or I'm taking you there myself.' I no longer had the strength to argue.

His blunt concern caught me off guard, and despite my protests that I was fine – just a bit overworked and under the weather – I could see the writing on the wall. I was no longer the master of my own fate; my body had staged a mutiny, and it was winning.

Breathing had become an extreme sport, each inhalation a Herculean effort. The cough was relentless, my lungs felt like they were being tickled by a feather that had obviously overstayed its welcome, insisting on a grand performance at the most inopportune moments. Fevers came and went like uninvited guests, their sweaty palms leaving their mark on my brow. It was a full-body experience, a carnival of discomfort, where the merry-go-round spun a tad too fast and the bumper cars had a vendetta against my poor, beleaguered ribcage.

So, there I was, being ferried to Trafford Hospital, the very place I had hoped to avoid. My initial hope was a prescription for some antibiotics, a few days' rest maybe. Surely a future Ironman couldn't be taken down that easily?

The doctor's diagnosis was a punch to the gut: bacterial pneumonia. It wasn't just a setback; it was a full stop. All those miles, all that training, all for nothing. My grand plans for Ironman UK crumbled like a house of cards in a gust of wind.

Chapter 3
The (Future) Iron Widow

At this point it's time to rewind even further, to find the real source of my Ironman fixation, and my first date with my future wife Briony.

Going back ten years, it was over a pint of Guinness for me and a gin and tonic for Briony that the seeds of my triathlon journey were unwittingly sown. On our first date, in a cosy pub in Clapham, London, the conversation took an unexpected dive into the world of triathlons. Briony, with the casualness of someone discussing the weather, mentioned she had signed up for a sprint triathlon in the Docklands, inspired by watching the Brownlee brothers at the 2012 London Olympics just a few short miles away from where we sat. The gin in her glass didn't swirl half as much as the idea in my head.

By the time our third date came around, and a budding romance was growing, Briony had shyly hinted at the possibility of me being her one-man support crew. Equally keen to impress her and wrapped up in the romance of it all, I agreed. I didn't just fall for her that day; I fell for the sport. The energy, the nerves, the unadulterated joy of crossing the finish line – it was infectious.

There's something undeniably cheeky about the name 'Virgin London Sprint Triathlon'. As if one is gently dipping a toe into the choppy waters of triathlons, still pure and untainted by the madness of full Ironman pursuits.

The swim segment was a splashy affair in the shadow of the O2 Arena, where Briony tried to channel the spirit of Michael Phelps while not ingesting too much of the Thames's 'essence'.

Then came the bike ride, a breezy tour through London's streets that felt suspiciously like a video game from my vantage point as I watched Briony dodging, weaving, and occasionally speeding past her fellow triathletes. The closed roads were a cyclist's dream, providing a fleeting fantasy of what commuting in the city could be like if cars were suddenly a thing of the past. Finally, the run, where Briony was cheered on by crowds that made you feel like you were leading the London Marathon – probably helped by the fact she was a young woman in Lycra.

As for me, after I had waved her off as she scampered to join her identikit wetsuit army, prepping for the swim start, I started to look round the event stalls. The gels, the shoes, the Lycra. Despite it not crossing my mind before, by the time I saw Briony race down the finishing chute with the biggest smile on her face, I fancied more than her that day.

Five years later, we had left London to travel around South America, and then decided to relocate to Manchester. It was Briony who nudged me towards my own start line as she signed me up for my debut in a sprint triathlon in Media City, consisting of a 750m swim, a 22km cycle and a 5km run. The day was baking hot, the kind of heat that had spectators fanning themselves with race programmes. I, on the other hand, was about to don a wetsuit and plunge into the open water of Salford Quays.

Briony's encouragement was a constant through it all. She had a knack for pushing me to my limits while making me believe it was exactly where I wanted to go. When I raised doubts about the open-water swim, her motivation became more than a little threatening – her message clear: I was doing it; no backing out! I emerged from the water with some of the finest front-crawl-meets-doggy-paddle technique.

I waddled like a penguin trying to free myself from the neoprene embrace of my wetsuit, and Briony was there, cheering me on and capturing the moment for posterity – and for a good laugh later. If you think this is an exaggeration, of the 500 or so participants that day, my tangle with the wetsuit made me the second slowest out of the transition area!

With every stroke and pedal, Briony was my unwavering supporter. She'd send me off with a smile and welcome me back after every completed lap of the bike course. Her positivity was the kind that could outshine the brightest of suns, and on the day of my first triathlon it was more refreshing than the aid stations.

Then there I was in Transition 2 (T2), wrangling my feet into running shoes like a contortionist at a talent show, post-bike legs wobbling like jelly on a jackhammer. This was Media City, the land of the BBC and ITV, where dreams are broadcast and, for one day, triathlons take centre stage. The transition area was a frenzy of Lycra-clad warriors, all swapping their cleats for trainers with more urgency than the contestants on the game shows being filmed next door. My prize was the ability to feel my toes again. I laced up, stood up and, with the grace of a new-born giraffe, stumbled forward to begin the run.

The route was a tour de force around Salford Quays, a concrete jungle where the water glistens with the reflections of digital dreams and soap opera storylines. Spectators lined the paths, offering cheers and possibly hoping to spot a *Coronation Street* star. Instead, they got to watch a parade of sweaty athletes, each one red-faced and determined, chugging along like steam trains on a mission.

Running past the iconic Lowry Theatre, I imagined the audience inside, enjoying culture and air conditioning, while I pounded the pavement, my own personal drama playing out with each step. The route took us by the Imperial War Museum North, a tribute to resilience, which I sorely needed, as my legs began to question life choices that had led to this moment.

Looping back towards Media City, the endorphins finally kicked in – or maybe it was just relief that the end was near. I could see the finish line now, a beacon of triumph in a sea of exhaustion, nestled in the heart of this broadcasting mecca.

Crossing the finish line, I was greeted not by a news anchor but by a medal-bearing volunteer, their smile as bright as the studio lights. The medal was heavy around my neck, a tangible reminder of the sprint through Media City. I stood there, medal clinking softly, in the epicentre of television greatness, a triumphant grin spreading across my face.

This wasn't just a race; it was a broadcast of human tenacity, and I had my own starring role in my very first triathlon. Lights, camera, action – I had sprinted, spun and splashed my way to glory in the Media City Sprint Triathlon.

I'd joke with Briony later, in the midst of my new-found triathlon obsession, 'You do realise whatever I sign up to next is all because of you, right?' Her laughter in response was light and free, the sound of someone who had no regrets about introducing their partner to what would become a shared passion. She had unknowingly created a monster.

Briony was there for the small victories, the near misses and the personal records. She didn't just tolerate my early morning training sessions and my ever-growing collection of race medals; she celebrated them. And when I wobbled across the finish line of that first sprint triathlon, it was Briony's face I searched for in the crowd.

She'd unwittingly created the (future) Iron Widow, a term we'd laugh about as we imagined a future where weekends were monopolised by my race training. But Briony didn't seem to mind; she thrived on the energy of the events and the community we'd become part of.

The journey from that first date to the finish line of my first sprint triathlon was a testament to the power of support and love. It wasn't just my legs propelling me forward; it was Briony's belief in me. She was the unsung hero of my triathlon tales, the woman behind the man who was slowly but surely becoming an Ironman.

Chapter 4
Finding Strength in Vulnerability

Back to the present day and the Ironman was well and truly off; there I was, feeling like a deflated balloon after a party. That's when Briony, with her infinite wisdom, suggested a holiday. 'Let's go get some sun,' she said. 'We'll get away over the weekend of the Ironman, put some physical and mental space between us and it.' The next thing I knew, we were booked for an all-inclusive in Turkey, swapping Manchester for the embrace of the Mediterranean sun, on what I liked to melodramatically call 'The Great Escape'.

Our destination? Antalya, where the sun shines as generously as a British granny offering biscuits, and all-inclusive hotels sprawl like sultans lounging on their divans. Boarding the flight at Manchester Airport, we squeezed into our seats, with knee space designed for a hobbit on a diet. As we landed, the warm air enveloped us like a toasty blanket, a stark contrast to the self-imposed glum that I had left behind. Antalya's airport bustled with the promise of adventure and Briony's eyes sparkled with the reflection of holiday website dreams coming to life. Our transfer to the hotel was a whirlwind of landscapes blurring past the window.

Then, the hotel. It sprawled before us like a mirage, an oasis of indulgence. We were greeted with a hospitality so warm it could have hatched eggs, ushered in with the promise of unlimited food, drink, and sun lounging – the holy trinity of vacation goals. The three things that could block out all memories of a failed swim, bike and run.

As we ventured out to explore the all-inclusive paradise, with its buffet tables groaning under the weight of more baclava than a royal feast, I knew one thing for certain – this was going to be a holiday to remember. Briony and I, flying from the familiar grey of Manchester to the golden embrace of Antalya, had traded triathlon training for a different kind of three disciplines: eat, swim, relax, repeat.

It wasn't just a holiday. It was a pilgrimage to find some semblance of peace after the chaos of the last few months. The insistence from Briony to take it slow bruised my ego somewhat – a reminder of the damage that had been done. She was right, as usual. The initial few days were about recovery, about learning to give myself grace and room to breathe without the pressure of training sessions and performance metrics looming over me.

The days were languid, a stark contrast to the regimented schedule I'd become accustomed to. They say still waters run deep, and in the stillness of those Turkish days I found a quiet kind of strength I hadn't known before. There were no training sessions, no early morning alarms, just the two of us, the open sky and an all-inclusive bar.

Getting the all-clear from the doctors back home to start light training again prior to boarding our flight had been the turning point. The X-rays showed no sign of long-term damage to my lungs: a clean bill of health that felt like a starting-gun in its own right. It was Briony who tempered my excitement with a gentle reminder: 'Baby steps,' she cautioned, her hand in mine, a silent vow that we were in this together.

And so, baby steps it was. The first run in the Turkish heat was nothing short of a revelation. The air was different here – hot, heavy and scented with the sea. Each breath was a mixture of salt and triumph. My legs, initially so unsure and shaky, began to remember their old strength, their old rhythm. It was just running, not training, a subtle but important distinction that Briony pointed out with a smile.

The holiday became a metaphor for recovery. The all-inclusive buffet was no longer about carb-loading but about savouring flavours. The pool was not for laps but for lazy drifts under the sun. Even the evening entertainment was a far cry from analysing race footage – it was about laughter and living in the moment.

But it was in those runs, under the Turkish sun, that the real healing happened. I wasn't clocking any good times or pushing myself in any significant way; I was simply moving, celebrating what my body could still do. Something that had previously felt so normal, felt that little bit more precious. Each drop of sweat was a testament to my resilience, each stride a promise that I was getting stronger, not just physically but mentally too.

Briony was there every step of the way, her encouragement now not so much a push but a steady presence. She cheered from the sun lounger every run, no matter how short and sweaty, and celebrated each day that I woke up feeling more like myself.

Finding strength in vulnerability wasn't just a chapter title; it was the theme of our getaway. I learned that there's courage in admitting you're not okay, that there's power in giving yourself time to heal, and that there's a special kind of joy in rediscovering your passion at a slower pace.

As our holiday in Turkey drew to a close, I found that I was looking forward to returning home with a new perspective. The Ironman might have been the initial goal, but what I had found was something far more valuable: the understanding that strength isn't just about enduring pain or pushing your body to its limits. Sometimes, it's about the quiet determination to start again, the willingness to listen to those who care for you, and the small, consistent steps towards recovery.

We packed our bags with more than just souvenirs; we packed memories of the journey we'd taken together. A pressure-free trip where I had learned to embrace rather than just push myself. This was a gift that I wouldn't have had if my best-laid plans of participating in the Ironman that year had come to fruition. As the plane took off, homeward bound, I realised that this holiday was more than a respite; it was the first chapter of a new beginning. And as the seatbelt sign turned off, I felt a weight lift off my shoulders – the weight of unmet expectations, of roads not taken and races not run. What lay ahead was unknown, but for the first time in a long while, that felt okay.

Chapter 5
Slowly but Surely

The rest of 2019 was a testament to the old adage: slow and steady wins the race – or in our case, completes the 10k without any dramatic fainting spells or desperate lunges for the nearest bench. Tatton Park saw us don our running shoes and as we lined up at the start; I glanced over at Briony, who was bouncing on the balls of her feet like an over-caffeinated kangaroo. 'Remember, it's not about the time,' she reminded me, though her twitching leg muscles told a different story. 'It's just about finishing.' She proceeded to set a pace that could best be described as 'optimistically sustainable' and finish we did, crossing the line with grins wider than the finishing banner.

Our regular runs around Manchester grew more frequent, and by this point we were seasoned pros – well, seasoned in the art of not collapsing, at least. We ran past landmarks and down streets that echoed with the hustle of city life, now repurposed as our running track. It was the high of recovery, of return and of shared victory.

Our running renaissance was interspersed with breaks that took us on adventures beyond the UK. Copenhagen was a highlight, with its waterside runs that felt like sprints through a postcard. We'd pass by the Little Mermaid statue, offering her silent encouragement, before rewarding ourselves with a trip to Tivoli Gardens.

Tivoli, with its old-world charm, was like stepping inside a snow globe, where the scent of roasted chestnuts wafted through the air, mingling with the sounds of festive tunes that made you want to waltz with the nearest stranger or lamppost. We wandered past stalls bursting with Christmas wares while cradling warm mulled wine. As we stared at the illuminated festive Ferris wheel, we couldn't help but be filled with seasonal charm and a refreshed vigour for life.

It was during these jaunts that I felt it – the unmistakable return to health. My lungs, once traitorous, now kept pace with my ambitions. My legs, formerly akin to overcooked spaghetti, now carried me with a vigour I remembered from my pre-pneumonia days. Each run was a celebration, each kilometre a silent toast to the resilience of the human body and spirit.

As 2019 drew to a close and 2020 started in earnest, we kicked off the year with a trip to the small island of Malta, with a half-marathon to participate in before tagging on a sunny celebration of our journey. The Malta experience was a blend of historical sightseeing and athletic endeavour, with race-day dawning bright and clear.

Briony and I found ourselves at the starting line of the Malta Half-Marathon, beneath a sky as blue as a cartoon sea. Malta, with its history steeped in the tales of knights and sieges, was about to witness a different kind of conquest – a horde of runners vying for personal glory on its sun-kissed streets.

The race was a point-to-point escapade from one side of the island to the other, a tour de force from Mdina, the silent city, to Sliema's bustling seafront. As the starting gun popped like a cork from a bottle of bubbly, we were off, our running shoes slapping the ancient cobblestones of Mdina with an eagerness that bordered on the indecent.

Mdina's fortified walls stood silent witness to our charge, their centuries-old stones unimpressed by our modern-day marathon madness. We weaved through the narrow streets, each twist and turn a step back in time, as if we were chasing the ghosts of knights past on their noble steeds – only our steeds were Nikes and Adidas.

Exiting the city's embrace, the route unfurled like a red carpet through Malta's heart, entering a more rural section where vineyards and olive groves flanked us as we raced forward. Past Rabat we ran, where locals cheered us on with the enthusiasm of football fans, their claps and hollers the wind beneath our beleaguered wings.

As we approached the coast, the Mediterranean Sea winked at us. The race morphed into a travelogue, with each mile showcasing Malta's eclectic blend of old and new. We darted past the Mosta Dome, its massive rotunda a silent scream of architectural marvel, and I half-wondered if we could take a quick detour for a touristy nose around.

The latter miles became a blur, like watching a documentary on fast-forward. Through the towns of Attard and Balzan we flew, our strides a rhythmic chant that spurred us on. The support was unwavering; children with outstretched hands waiting for high-fives became our honorary coaches, their giggles a symphony that played the soundtrack of our endeavour.

Finally, Sliema beckoned, the finish line drawing us in like a lighthouse for weary ships. Crossing it in the now blazing sunshine was a moment of euphoria, the kind that warrants a freeze-frame and a triumphant power ballad. The medal placed around our necks felt like a knighthood, the weight of it a tangible reminder of the journey, the sights, the sounds and the soul of Malta we'd carried with us every step of the way.

Amid the celebrations, however, a whisper began to circulate – a whisper that grew into a murmur and then a conversation. Covid-19 had started to become an increasingly common topic. A virus, potentially serious, was making headlines. At this point the only impact on the race had been the blanket ban on any athletes travelling from northern Italy – the European hotbed for Covid in those early days. There on the sun-drenched streets of Malta, it seemed distant, a concern for another day.

Returning to the UK, the whisper had become a shout. We touched down to news of lockdowns, of a world bracing for uncertainty. The jubilation of our Maltese adventure was quickly overshadowed by a sense of foreboding. The streets that had welcomed our running strides now felt eerily still, and a future trip for the Lisbon half marathon in a couple of weeks was immediately parked.

As the announcement of the lockdown was made, Briony and I sat in our living room, the medals from Malta hanging mockingly on the wall. The future was uncertain, the races all cancelled, the parks closed. But we had each other, and we had our health, hard-won as it was.

The chapter of our lives marked by the joy of running was closing, at least for now. But we knew that the strength we had found in each other, in the recovery and in the miles we had covered together, would carry us through the days ahead.

So, we waited, in a world suddenly paused, holding on to the hope that this was just an intermission, not the end of the show. Because if there was one thing we had learned, it was that no matter how slowly you go, as long as you do not stop, you'll get where you need to be. And sometimes, as painful as it may be, where you need to be is right where you are – at home, sheltered from the world outside.

Chapter 6
The Email

And so, as lockdown began in the UK, amongst clapping for heroes and racing for food delivery slots, we, like many, converted our little kitchen into a new work-from-home office, where every day turned into a 'bring your cat to work' day. As the world donned lounge wear and perfected the art of the mute button, an email from Ironman UK landed in my inbox with the subtlety of a bull in a Zoom meeting.

As I clicked open the email, a reminder from a pre-pandemic era, I braced myself for its contents, expecting the usual clang of embarrassment about past failures. It was a reminder of goals set in a time when hand sanitiser and toilet rolls weren't deemed valuable currency and 'social distancing' was just poor party etiquette. Little did I know what this digital note was about to trigger:

> Dear Athlete,
> We appreciate your continued patience and understanding while we have been working through potential race options for you after previously confirming that the IRONMAN UK triathlon, originally scheduled for July 12 cannot take place in 2020 and will return on July 4, 2021.
> All registered athletes of the 2020 IRONMAN UK triathlon will have their race registration automatically deferred to the 2021 race date, but we have also provided additional race options if you are unable to race on July 4, 2021.

* * *

There it was, an electronic relic from a past life where DNS (Did Not Start) was the label slapped across my triathlon dreams. The 2019 Ironman UK, with its siren call, had been a no-go, and I'd shoved that disappointment into the same dusty corner of my mind. But now it was back, popping up in my inbox like a jack-in-the-box I never wanted to crank.

The email was oddly out of place amongst the daily onslaught of sales alerts and invites to yet more virtual quizzes. I'd forgotten that at the last minute in 2019, when pneumonia hit, I had deferred my inexplicably expensive Ironman entry to 2020 on medical grounds. To be honest, I'd then written off the possibility of taking part in 2020, feeling I had as much chance of mastering quantum physics or resisting Briony's lockdown baking.

Staring at the screen, I mulled over the past months. The thrill of completing 10ks together in Tatton Park and Manchester, the camaraderie, the shared fatigue – it all seemed a lifetime ago. And then there was Copenhagen, running along the waterside, the city a blur of Danish design and the warmth of mulled wine tingling in our veins.

Yet here I was, with the opportunity to go toe-to-toe with the Ironman once more, and I couldn't decide whether it was a sign or a cosmic joke. Had I not been vocally certain, last year, that my chances of being fit for the next Ironman were as slim as finding a snowflake in the Sahara? But here was the opportunity. I had a free hit at 2021.

I sat, the email open, the cursor blinking like a heartbeat on the screen. To everyone else, my Ironman journey had ended with a DNS – Did Not Start – that much-discussed, little-understood acronym that felt like a badge of defeat. To try again would be to step back into the arena where I'd once fallen, to risk once more potential embarrassment in front of friends and family, to lay bare the hope that I'd carefully reconstructed.

The Ironman had always been more than a race; it was a dream, a measure of my recovery, a testament to my will. And now, as the world braced against the Covid-19 virus, as conversations became peppered with words like 'pandemic' and 'quarantine', that dream flickered once more.

I closed the email, the offer hanging in the digital ether. The decision loomed large, not just a tick-box on a race form but a question of what I wanted my story to be. Did I dare to chase the Ironman finish line again, to train for the joy of it amidst a world paused by fear?

As Briony and I packed away the last of the holiday gear and settled back into the routine of home life, the decision weighed on me. I knew, deep down, that the Ironman was calling, a challenge whispering through the uncertainty of locked-down days.

The chapter closed not with a bang, but with the soft click of a laptop shutting. I was left with my thoughts, the quiet of the house and the lingering scent of cakes – a sweet reminder of normality. The Ironman UK was a chance at redemption, at proving to myself that I could rise from the ashes of a DNS. Whether I took that chance remained to be seen, but as I looked at the empty cake platter, I realised that sometimes it's not all about getting to the finish line; it's about having the courage to start.

Chapter 7
What is Ironman?

At this juncture, a light bulb pops on, and it occurs to me – I've prattled on about this impending Ironman like it's a Sunday stroll when, in fact, some may think it's a new Tony Stark release. So, let's set the record straight: what, pray tell, is an Ironman Triathlon?

Imagine, if you will, a day that starts with a 2.4-mile swim in waters often so chilly they could make a polar bear shiver. That's just for starters, like the amuse-bouche of a very, very long banquet. Once you've crawled from the brine, you hop on to what we hope is a trusty steed (of the two-wheeled variety) for a 112-mile cycling jaunt through hills, dales and possibly a mini-tornado, because, well, Mother Nature loves a good show.

At this point you're done, right? Just when your legs start penning their resignation letter, it's time to run a marathon. That's right, a full 26.2-mile marathon. A proper marathon full of the usual blood, sweat and tears.

Now, the Ironman Triathlon isn't just some modern masochistic ritual. No, it has roots. Born in the late 1970s in Hawaii, it was the brainchild of Navy Commander John Collins. Picture this: a group of friends, likely with moustaches billowing in the Pacific breeze, debating which athletes were the fittest – swimmers, cyclists or runners. Collins, possibly with a twinkle in his eye, suggested combining the three long-distance events already happening on the island. And like that, the Ironman was conceived, less out of science and more out of a 'hold my beer' macho moment.

The distances, arguably, were not a result of science or consideration of what is humanly possible. Instead, the Waikiki Roughwater Swim, the Around-Oahu Bike Race (shortened for sanity's sake), and the Honolulu Marathon were strung together in a challenge so formidable that merely finishing would be a badge of honour.

And the cut-offs? Oh, the cut-offs. You have 17 hours to go from start to glorious finish. The clock is as unforgiving as a parking inspector. Miss the cut-off time in the swim, and your day is done before you've even had a chance to chafe on the bike. Linger too long in the transition, affectionately known as T1 (where you morph from aquatic creature to land cyclist), and you might as well be turning pumpkins into carriages.

The bike cut-off is no less stern. You must be off your bicycle before the sun dips below the horizon. Then there's the marathon, where the cut-off times are the dangling carrot to keep you running, jogging or crawling towards that finish line.

Let's not gloss over the transitions, either. T1 is where you realise that peeling off a wetsuit gracefully is an art form unto itself, and T2 (the bike-to-run switch) often feels like a quick-change act in a talent show you never signed up for.

Now, why would anyone voluntarily sign up for this festival of endurance, you ask? It's not just for the free gels and the shiny medal at the end. No, there's a certain *je ne sais quoi* about testing the limits of human endurance, of finding out what you're made of, and of having stories that start with, 'This one time, during an Ironman …'

So, as you embark on reading the riotous and heartfelt tale of *Tri Again*, let this chapter serve as a primer to the sheer madness and magnificence of the Ironman Triathlon. It's not just a race; it's a pilgrimage to the extremes of sport and life itself, a testament to the power of human will, and quite possibly the best worst idea anyone ever had.

At this point, *surely* I have convinced you to join me on this mad adventure they call Ironman, right? So, you've just got to pick your destination of choice for this madcap adventure. Ironman Barcelona – where you can at least stare at some amazing architecture? No. Ironman Nice – where you can at least guarantee the weather for post recovery? No. Maybe the Ironman mecca that is Hamburg? No. My Ironman of choice was 40 minutes up the road in Bolton, where they host Ironman UK.

Ironman UK, the jewel in Bolton's otherwise un-sparkly athletic crown (sorry to all you Bolton Wanderers fans out there). Nestled in the heart of the land where pies are king and the word 'grim' is a term of endearment, Ironman UK is an event that laughs in the face of the word 'daunting'.

Bolton, with its proud industrial heritage and a penchant for inclement weather that would make even the most seasoned weatherman weep, is the perfect setting for such an ordeal. Here, the course isn't just a course; it's a character in its own right, complete with mood swings and dramatic flair.

The swim takes place in the flashily named Pennington Flash, a body of water that sounds like a superhero but feels more like a super-villain when you're slicing through its often-chilly embrace at the crack of dawn. Emergence from this aquatic escapade is met with cheers, relief and the more than occasional swan spectator giving you the side-eye. Bear in mind, this is the lake that is credited for gifting me bacterial pneumonia first time around.

Then there's the bike course, a 112-mile ride that is famous for its constant hills, rubbish road surfaces, tight corners and high rates of casualties. Did I mention the hills? The inclines have reduced grown men and women to tears. It's not enough to ride the route once; oh no, you must conquer it three times, proving your worth to the triathlon gods and the local sheep population that watches with judgemental eyes.

Then let's not forget the marathon, where you're greeted by the sort of crowds that make you wonder if The Beatles have reunited just up the road. The locals turn out in force, offering encouragement, jelly babies and the sort of banter that can only be honed in the North of England. Four laps of Bolton, with a dramatic incline through Queens Park that will drag anyone still running to their knees (or at least a slow walk).

Ironman UK in Bolton is a beast, a challenge that demands respect, whether you're a first-timer or a seasoned pro. It's a course where every inch gained is a victory, and every mile completed is a story to regale your grandkids with (or anyone who'll listen as you recount the tale for the umpteenth time).

Welcome to Bolton, where the Ironman dream is as tough and gratifying as a hot pot on a rainy day.

Chapter 8
The Decision

Lockdown life was an endless loop of Zoom meetings, where colleagues morphed into pixelated versions of themselves, and virtual quizzes, which became the new Friday night out. My daily existence was punctuated by the 'ping' of calendar reminders for events that no longer existed, and the scramble for food delivery slots was the new supermarket sweep.

Amidst this new routine, the canal towpath became my sanctuary. Every lunchtime, without fail, I'd lace up the running shoes and hit the path, nodding at the usual suspects: the joggers, the dog walkers, and those ducks, who I swear were judging my form. I fell into a rhythm, the monotony of lockdown offset by the simple act of putting one foot in front of the other.

I entered the Cheshire Half-Marathon, set to take place in September 2020, and the months leading up to it were a mix of endorphin-fuelled highs and muscle-aching lows. The runs weren't just about keeping fit; they were about keeping sane. Each stride was a silent rebellion against the claustrophobia of quarantine, each mile a testament to the determination to emerge from this pandemic not just unscathed, but stronger. It was also a reminder of a world where we took our freedom for granted, where the ability to travel was a given. A reminder these basic human rights we assume will always be there should have been appreciated.

As the half-marathon approached, the reality of racing again started to sink in. The prospect of swapping the solitude of the canal for the return to a collective start-line buzz was both exhilarating and terrifying. But as I stood at the majestic Capesthorne Hall, with its sprawling grounds now a socially distanced race track, excitement won out.

The air was electric with the collective energy of runners, all of us a cocktail of nerves, hand sanitiser and discarded face masks. As I crossed the start line at the Cheshire Half-Marathon, the grandeur of Capesthorne Hall loomed over the runners like a benevolent overlord, bidding us peasants to run for glory on its lavish lands.

The route was as quintessentially British as a cup of tea with the Queen. We spilled out from the Hall's gates like a scene from Downton Abbey if the aristocratic family had taken up jogging. Our trainers kissed the tarmac, imprinting the hopes and dreams of every runner on to the picturesque roads of the Cheshire plains.

Onward we surged, past fields dotted with lazy, grazing sheep, who eyed us with the disinterest only a creature born to chew cud can muster. The rolling hills were less 'rolling' and more 'undulating' with a cheeky incline here and there to test our mettle and our calves.

The halfway point came and went, marked by a water station that resembled a pit stop at the Grand Prix, masked volunteers brandishing water bottles like they were bestowing knighthoods. A quick sip and we were off again, chasing down the second half with the determination you'd expected from a group of runners who had been denied their running fix for the past six months.

The roads of Siddington and Marton bowed to our will, each mile conquered adding to the growing legend of our athletic quest. Spectators were few and far between, a reminder that this was one of the first few events back after a prolonged period of isolation and we were not back to normal just yet. The silence beyond the slapping of trainers against the tarmac a reminder that this was very much a solo endeavour.

As the finish line back at Capesthorne Hall came into view, a surge of adrenaline coursed through my veins. I was no longer just a participant; I was a contender, a dark horse galloping towards a personal victory that had seemed so elusive at the start.

I crossed the line with the clock stopping at a triumphant 1:37:32, a new personal best. The time was a revelation, a clear sign of what months of canal-side runs could culminate in. There was no medal ceremony, no crowds to high-five, thanks to this being a pared-back first mass participation event – just the quiet pride of personal victory amidst the oddity of our socially distanced reality.

The post-race glow stayed with me as I returned to the world of Zoom and remote work. The tedium of lockdown was now interspersed with training recaps and recovery plans. The once-dreaded virtual quizzes became opportunities to boast about my latest running escapade, and the battle for grocery delivery slots turned into strategic planning sessions akin to military operations.

Yet, it was during these long, home-bound days that the decision took root. I had achieved something in that half-marathon, even amid unprecedented global upheaval. If I could do that, surely I could take on the Ironman. The thought was a thrill during the sting of cabin fever.

I would do it properly this time, with a coach who could channel the wild energy of my past training into a structured programme. No more guessing games with pacing or nutrition. I was ready to graduate from a solitary lone wolf to an Ironman-in-training, surrounded by a team and, if possible, allies.

As I closed my laptop on another virtual meeting, I felt the fire of anticipation. I was on the cusp of something big. The decision had been made. Ironman 2021, I was coming for you.

With the decision made, the coach hunt began in earnest. I scoured the internet, read reviews and sat through more Zoom meetings, this time with prospective trainers. I wasn't looking for a drill sergeant; I wanted a mentor, someone to harness my enthusiasm and guide it towards that elusive finish line.

As lockdown life dragged on, my Ironman dream became a beacon of hope. It was a goal that stretched beyond the confines of my kitchen-turned-office, beyond the canal towpath and into the realm of possibility. It was a challenge that whispered of a return to a life where social distancing was a choice, not a mandate.

Chapter 9
The Coach Who Believed

In the not-so-splendid isolation of a British lockdown, finding Coach Garrie felt like discovering a rare coin down the back of the sofa. I had first seen him at an open-water event, on the day I'd later come to know as 'the pneumonia plunge'. There he was, the triathlon sage, doling out advice with the patience of a saint and the precision of an engineer to a group of fellow Ironman wannabes.

Months later, as I scrolled the internet for possible coaches with Ironman experience, Coach Garrie's name surfaced from the depths of my memory. A quick digital pilgrimage through the hallowed pages of his website confirmed my suspicions: Coach Garrie was the real deal. His record of Ironman triumphs was as long and distinguished as a Beefeater's tenure at the Tower of London. Since finishing his debut triathlon in 1990, Coach Garrie had completed over 250 events over every distance, including Ironman, and had many a podium finish to bolster his CV.

Our first virtual meeting had all the awkwardness of a blind date. I fumbled through my athletic history like a nervous teenager, while Coach Garrie watched with the patience of a saint – or perhaps a cat eyeing a particularly slow mouse. When I mentioned my goal, his eyebrows shot up so high they nearly left his forehead. 'Ironman UK 2021?' he echoed, his tone a mixture of disbelief and intrigue.

As I continued, Coach Garrie's face was an enigma, betraying nothing as I charted my aspirations to tackle Ironman UK 2021. When I finished, there was a pause so pregnant with anticipation it could have birthed quintuplets. 'Ironman UK 2021, eh?' he repeated, each syllable carrying the weight of northern gravitas.

The conversation shifted gears as Coach Garrie recounted his own experiences. He wasn't showing off; he was illustrating the map of where I wanted to go, having navigated its contours himself. His tales weren't just about crossing finish lines; they were about the mud, sweat and gears – the grit of the journey.

When we drilled down to my fitness levels, Coach Garrie's questions were like a professor's pop quiz. 'VO2 max? Thresholds? Spit it out,' he prodded. I relayed my stats, feeling like a contestant on *University Challenge* pressing the buzzer with trepidation and feeling well out of my depth.

Coach Garrie's approach was like a British bulldog – tenacious, determined and unforgiving. He chewed over my training plan like a tough steak, dissecting and evaluating with a critic's eye. 'Your regime is as organised as a car boot sale,' he chuckled, making mental notes to upend my chaotic approach to training.

Yet, for all his gruff exterior, Coach Garrie agreed to take me on. It was a handshake deal over cyberspace, my screen glowing with the promise of a fresh start. 'I'll whip you into shape,' he assured me, and I had no doubt he would – or I'd die as we tried.

Our training sessions became the stuff of legend. Coach Garrie didn't coddle; he challenged. My form was picked apart like a contestant on *The Great British Bake Off*, but every pointed critique came with a side order of wisdom. Behind every one of Coach Garrie's brusque assessments was the unshakeable belief that we could do this.

As the autumn leaves began to carpet the ground, a decision had been forged in the fires of Coach Garrie's no-nonsense coaching style. I was going to tackle Ironman, and I was going to do it under the wing of a man who'd seen more finish lines than a London cab driver had seen traffic jams.

After finishing my call and sitting back from my computer, I couldn't help but feel a surge of excitement. To do it properly this time, that was the mantra. With Coach Garrie's guidance, 'properly' felt within reach, as tangible as the medal that would one day hang around my neck. I've always been a person who finds comfort in a plan, in numbers. Yet this is where I went drastically wrong first time around. Now, the coach who believed had extended his hand, and I had grasped it firmly. It was time to get to work.

Chapter 10

The Two-Wheeled Steed

A wetsuit and new running shoes were on the agenda, but with running miles already in the bank and the British weather making outdoor swimming unlikely till early spring, priority one was clear – I needed a new bike. A chariot worthy of the Ironman challenge. One does not simply pedal into Bolton; one must be equipped with a mechanical steed that scoffs at hills and snickers at headwinds. Okay, at least one that would give me a fighting chance against the raging hills and an eight-hour cut-off.

The great debate unfurled – road bike or tri bike? The road bike, with its versatility and friendly geometry, beckoned with the promise of a comfortable ride through the undulating landscapes of the North. The tri bike, with its aggressive stance and aerodynamic lines, whispered sweet nothings of speed and efficiency. But the visions of charging up Bolton's hills on a tri bike, with its handlebars low like a moody teenager, quickly turned to thoughts of my quads weeping. That, and I am a Yorkshireman by birth, and the longevity and usage of a road bike trumped the likely short-term usage of a fancy tri bike. And so, practicality won – a road bike it would be, one that could tackle ascents like a mountain goat on caffeine.

Next was the conundrum of make and model. Should I go for the Italian flair of a Bianchi, the steadfast reliability of a Specialized, or the aerodynamic wizardry of a Cervélo? In the end, I returned to an old friend – a Boardman.

Ah, Boardman – the brand that rolls off the tongue as smoothly as their bikes glide over tarmac. Conceived by cycling royalty, Chris Boardman himself, Olympian and wearer of the yellow jersey, it's a name that conjures visions of speed, precision and a touch of British flair. These bikes are not mere carbon concoctions; they are the steeds of weekend warriors and aspiring triathletes, each model infused with the spirit of competition and a dollop of 'keep calm and pedal on'. It's the everyman's answer to a pro-level experience, delivering performance that can make you feel like a contender, even if you're just sprinting for the village sign. Also, they provide some of the best bang for your buck in the cycling world – did I mention I am a Yorkshireman?

So, after seven years' service it was time to retire my trusty old Boardman, to be replaced by its younger, fresher brother. This one would have a carbon frame, as light as my hopes and dreams, ready to slice through the air like a hot knife through butter.

With my decision made, it was time for the hunt to begin. The internet became my savannah, and I, a persistent predator, stalking through pages of listings, stacking voucher codes and firing off eBay bids in the hope of snagging my perfect partner in crime. It was during this digital safari that I spotted it – the perfect Boardman, barely used, at a price so good it felt like daylight robbery without the guilt.

There it was, nestled among listings of bikes that had seen more action than a James Bond film, the eBay listing that made my heart skip a gear. 'Like New Boardman Road Bike – Manchester Pickup Only' it declared. Ruling out many who were unwilling to travel to pick up their potential new bike, it was the perfect set-up for a Manchester local with a penchant for two-wheeled bargains.

It was as if the cycling gods had crafted an advert just for me. The frame size was a match so perfect I half-expected fairy godmothers to appear offering sponsorship deals. Used only twice, it whispered of Sunday rides cut short, of a road not taken, and now it was beckoning me to write its next chapter.

And the extras! A pump to breathe life into tyres, lights that promised to guide me through the darkest training sessions, all thrown in with the casual generosity of a street magician pulling coins from behind ears. All this, for half the recommended retail price?

What could go wrong? This was eBay, the digital Wild West of ecommerce, where every 'Pay Now' click was a roll of the dice. Yet there it was, a listing so tantalising, so serendipitously suited to my needs, it felt less like a gamble and more like destiny. Too good to be true? Perhaps. But in the pursuit of Ironman glory, wasn't it worth chancing fate? After all, fortune favours the bold – or at least the quick to click.

But there it was; immediately after payment, the address revealed itself and I had found the catch – the bike was in Salford. For the uninitiated, you may associate Salford with the glamorous location of my first sprint triathlon adventure. Media City, shining like a beacon of modernity – home to the BBC, ITV and the Lowry Theatre. However, on the other side of Salford, well, let's just say it's got character in spades. The listing was in the latter, and a quick Google Streetview search made me question the legitimacy of carbon bikes being discarded at bargain prices after just a few rides.

With trepidation and excitement doing the tango in my stomach, I ventured forth the next evening to collect my prize. The address led me to a street so quiet you could hear the tension crackling in the air. Parking my car, I approached the house nervously, half expecting to be greeted by a troll demanding a riddle answer, or something a little more sinister.

Instead, a friendly chap answered the door, the bike in mint condition behind him. He spun a tale of impulse-buying with his company's bike-to-work scheme. But after two debut rides and the fear of pedalling with his feet clipped to pedals whilst facing Manchester rush hour traffic, he had a subsequent revelation of his true calling – the call of the wild, the untamed beauty of mountain biking. Safer, quieter and, let's face it, much more sensible than what I had planned.

As I wheeled my new companion back to the car, championing the result of my positive mental thinking, I found something quite odd – someone had parked right behind me. Odd as we were the only two cars on the street. And as much as I tried, they were parked just too close to fire open my boot, carefully place my Boardman inside and hit the road. Was this the plan all along? Had I been the 48th sucker to fall for this bargain eBay listing?

And so, with my heart beating fast, I perched the bike against the wall, and with a pace that Coach Garrie would be proud of, edged my car forward six feet before racing back to my new carbon best friend. Every second felt like an eternity, as I half-expected this to be the most elaborate bike theft scheme in history. But no, fortune smiled upon me that day, and with the bike finally nestled in the boot of my car, I made my getaway, leaving Salford with a prize catch and a heart still racing from the thrill of the bargain hunt.

The Boardman was home, a carbon-fibre promise of Ironman potential. As I leaned it against the shed wall, I couldn't help but admire its sleek lines and imagine the miles we'd cover together. This wasn't just a bike; it was a declaration, a testament and investment into the journey ahead, and the unorthodox path I'd taken to get it. It was a victory – not over any competitor, but over the trials of purchasing the one item that might just see me through to the finish line of the most significant race of my life.

Chapter 11

The Masterplan

The transition from the glorious lethargy of lockdown to the disciplined rigour of Coach Garrie's masterplan was, to put it mildly, a shock to the system. November heralded this new era with the subtlety of a brass band crashing through my front door.

Despite being based only 30 miles away, lockdown would restrict face to face time between me and my coach. Training for an Ironman was tough normally, but throw in a pandemic and a lockdown and it was set to be even more challenging. Thankfully, Coach Garrie had a solution to monitoring my progress. In the digital age of sweat and gears, my introduction to Training Peaks and Zwift was akin to Alice tumbling down the rabbit hole and finding herself in a wonderland of pixels and performance metrics.

Training Peaks became my new digital overlord, a platform where workouts were not just recorded, but analysed with the kind of scrutiny usually reserved for decoding the Rosetta Stone. A big flash of red for failed sessions would haunt me, but a sea of green when a session was completed made me feel oddly calm.

Meanwhile, Zwift turned my spare room into a virtual velodrome, a fantasy land where I could cycle through digital utopias, racing against avatars who represented real people in their own living rooms-cum-training camps. It was a place where I could climb alpine hills while actually just sweating profusely on to my carpet. No open roads for me in the short term, but with Zwift and Coach Garrie's training sessions there were to be no excuses.

Together, these platforms transformed my training. Along with my trusty Garmin for my run sessions, every pedal stroke and stride was logged, dissected and used to plot the downfall of my next personal best. It was training, but not as I knew it; it was training for the space age, and I was boldly going where many athletes had gone before, but now with more graphs, stats and a peloton of pixelated pals.

The 'base phase' as it was known was to build up my basic level of fitness pre-Christmas so we could push on in the new year. After an initial week of fitness tests, heart-rate readings and thresholds, the real fun began. Every other morning, as dawn cracked, I would find myself lacing up, half in anticipation, half in dread. The pavements became my proving grounds, and every passer-by a witness to my huffing transformation. Every other evening, I returned to my new Carbon Steed (my Boardman bicycle) mounted on my turbo trainer ready to pedal round the mythical streets on Zwift. You see, Coach Garrie's blueprint for Ironman glory was no mere suggestion; it was a decree, each session carved in stone tablets of sweat and toil.

Indoor cycling sessions on Zwift transformed my trusty two-wheeler into a steed of battle. I'd charge through virtual landscapes, climbing pixelated hills with the ferocity of a knight in a Monty Python sketch – valiant, if not a bit silly in hindsight. Coach Garrie's presence was ethereal, a voice over the speaker that could be both a balm and a cattle prod.

Every few days, his feedback would trickle through, the good, the bad and often the downright ugly, especially when it came to my technique. Often it was blunt, especially in the early days when I missed the odd session, when the temptation of reopening pubs and cosy evenings crept in. 'Get back home, you have a cycle session to make up,' came the coach's words on my WhatsApp. I reluctantly peeled away and returned to the turbo trainer, which looked on mockingly. And pedal I did, with the relentless gusto of a man on a mission, or at least a man who desperately didn't want to be caught in Coach Garrie's wrath.

The runs were a saga in themselves. Each one a chapter, they told the tale of a man slowly but surely reclaiming his fitness. The weekly hill sprints became a source of legend in my own mind. I tackled each incline with the grim determination of someone who'd been told the pubs would close if he didn't reach the summit in time. Pre Ironman training, my running had been on the lovely flats of Manchester. But Bolton had hills, so I had to prepare, no excuses allowed.

By the time December's chill had wrapped its icy fingers around the country, I had settled into a routine. The slow sessions, which Coach Garrie promised were building my 'base', felt less like foundation laying and more like constructing the entire ground floor. I was the architect of my own agony, drafting plans for a future where my legs didn't feel like lead weights at the end of a run.

Yet, with each passing day, I felt stronger. The runs along the canal, where once I'd stopped to catch my breath and admire the ducks, now saw me nodding at them in camaraderie as I sped past. 'Morning, chaps,' I'd puff, and I swear they quacked in encouragement. The base was being built.

Covid restrictions meant pool time was as rare as a dry day in Manchester, so I embraced the alternative with a passion reserved for substitute teachers. I spent hours watching YouTube guides on total immersion swimming, and any other tricks or tips I could learn ahead of my return to the water.

But the training wasn't all about the grind. Life during lockdown had its lighter moments. Zoom calls with friends became quiz nights where the only sports questions involved guessing how many kilometres I'd run that week. My family learned to gauge the success of my training by the volume of my post-workout groaning. 'Sounds like he did the hill runs today,' they'd chuckle from a safe distance.

As I cycled indoors, I'd daydream of races past and future. The drone of the bike trainer became a meditative hum, the perfect soundtrack to my visualisations of crossing the Ironman finish line, a dream that grew clearer with every session.

Mid-December arrived with the stealth of Santa on Christmas Eve, and with it, a sense of completion. The foundation level of fitness Coach Garrie had promised was no longer a mythical concept; it was real, as tangible as the Christmas pudding I was determined to avoid until race weight was achieved.

That first chapter closed with me, bike trainer silent for the evening, running shoes neatly paired by the door, ready for the next day's outing. The masterplan was well underway, a labour of love (and a fair bit of cursing), all guided by the occasionally heard but always felt presence of Coach Garrie.

'To do it properly this time,' I mused, the mantra becoming my own. Mid-December marked not just the end of the chapter but the beginning of the true test. Now, with a foundation as solid as a Christmas fruitcake, it was time to build towards the pinnacle of my training. The masterplan was in motion, the architect ready, the blueprints set. Ironman, I was on my way.

Chapter 12
Meeting Max

There's a certain breed of person who throws themselves into the fires of challenge, not just to be forged anew, but because they seem to genuinely enjoy the heat. Max is one such individual – a man whose LinkedIn profile is a tapestry woven with the threads of athletic prowess, business acumen and a genuinely lovely person.

His posts on LinkedIn are the stuff of legend, often extolling the virtues of 'doing hard things'. It is like motivational speaking meets corporate networking, and it works. One particular post on LinkedIn caught my eye for obvious reasons: a picture of Max, all smiles, announcing his intent to compete in Ironman UK in 2021.

Max is the epitome of 'annoyingly athletic'. He is the kind of guy you want to dislike purely on principle. Successful? Check. Family man with a heart of gold? Check. Taller than me by a good half foot? Double check. Yet, for all the reasons he can irk an average Joe, Max is as likeable as they come – a beacon of positivity with a knack for making you feel like you can run through walls, probably because he's already run through a few himself.

On a whim, after finding him on LinkedIn, I fired off a message. 'Hey, I'm doing Ironman too,' I typed, feeling like a small fish swimming up to a very shiny, very accomplished shark. To my surprise, Max messaged back almost immediately, his digital enthusiasm leaping off the screen. Not only did he offer words of encouragement, but he also suggested we meet up. 'Let's join forces,' he said, and I couldn't help but feel like I'd just been drafted into the Avengers.

Our first meeting was in person, socially distanced at a park that had become my second home. Max, true to form, went in for a hug – the kind that said 'we're in this together' – before remembering the protocol and awkwardly converting it into a sort of jazz-handed air embrace. From that moment, Max wasn't just a connection; he became a brother-in-arms.

Our conversations flowed like a well-organised race; there was no awkward shuffling, no fumbling for topics. We covered everything from training schedules to the philosophical musings that only long-distance running can inspire. Max was a wellspring of tips and strategies, freely given with the generosity of someone who knows that success is best shared. However, it was paired with a genuine openness and vulnerability; here we both were, on the brink of something so physically incomprehensible, 2.4 miles of icy lake, 112 miles of Bolton hills and then the toughest marathon either of us had ever faced.

He was an unexpected ally in the war against Ironman. Where I had Coach Garrie's gruff guidance, Max brought a cheerleader's spirit wrapped in the body of a true triathlete. He was the positive charge to my sometimes-negative ion, the guy who could spin a yarn about his latest adventure and leave you feeling like you were right there with him.

While we largely trained individually, the feedback and communication flowed. And now and then we'd reunite for a debrief and catch-up run. Those sessions became a thing of beauty, as we had each found someone who wouldn't tire of discussions around heart rates and energy gels. Max had the uncanny ability to turn even the most gruelling workout into an event worth attending. We'd push each other to the limits, finding camaraderie in the shared burn of lactic acid and the mutual understanding that pain was just weakness leaving the body – or in Max's case, probably just boredom.

As the weeks of training turned into months, I found myself drawing not just on Coach Garrie's tactical expertise, but also on Max's infectious optimism. He'd regale me with tales of his family, how they cheered him on. When the December chill set in, marking the tail-end of the year and the heart of our training, it was Max's unflagging spirit that kept the cold at bay as we were united by a common goal: Ironman UK.

We embarked on a brisk 10k run, our heart-rates nestled snugly in the cosy embrace of zone two – where the beats per minute are just enough to make you feel alive, but not enough to summon the Grim Reaper. We set off, our breaths fogging up our Garmin screens as we checked our heart-rate readings, ensuring we were in the Goldilocks zone – not too hard, not too soft, just right. This is the endurance runner's waltz, a delicate dance where one misstep could send you spiralling into the anaerobic abyss, a place where lactic acid flows more freely than words at a poetry slam.

We swapped the early war-stories of our first training blocks, comparing and contrasting our coaches' techniques, and passing on the rumours we'd heard about potential course adjustments. As we rounded the final corner of our planned route, the reality of our shared goal loomed ahead. Ironman was no longer a distant speck on the horizon; it was a mountain we were steadily climbing, each zone-two run a step further towards the summit.

Max grinned, clapping a hand on my shoulder. 'We've got this,' he assured me, and I believed him. Max was more than an unexpected ally; he was the reinforcement I hadn't known I needed. Together, we'd face the Ironman – two men against the course, against our own limitations, against anything life threw our way. With Max in my corner, the war seemed now winnable and victory that much sweeter.

Chapter 13
Christmas Build-Up and the Athlete's Advent

T'was the build-up to Christmas, and all through the house, not a creature was stirring, not even my desire to lounge on the couch. December 2020 had arrived with the stealth of a cat burglar, and with it a festive season which this year was to be masked and socially distanced. The usual temptations of Christmas markets and raucous office parties were replaced by the gentle hum of my indoor bike trainer, thanks in part to a new wave of government restrictions.

The rhythm of training had settled into me like a well-loved carol. Each session, whether it was a brisk jaunt through a frosty morning on the canal path or my latest sweat-inducing trip on the turbo trainer, was like an advent calendar of exertion, where instead of chocolates I was rewarded with a satisfying fatigue and the growing sense that maybe, just maybe, I could become an Ironman.

My weekly training schedule was a meticulously planned five to six hours, a carefully choreographed ballet of four or five sessions, and I was the principal dancer. The usual Yuletide temptations – mince pies, mulled wine and the siren call of lazy lie-ins – were rationed with a new-found dedication. In fact, I missed only two sessions all month, a testament to the burgeoning commitment to my Ironman cause over my usual burgeoning waistline at this time of year.

Even my Christmas list had undergone a transformation. Gone were the requests for the latest gadgets and crates of ale, replaced by the practical charm of energy gels, run socks and puncture-resistant inner tubes. Family members, bemused by my wish list, exchanged knowing glances and mocking messages as they attempted to wrap up tubes of carbohydrate tablets and folded rubber tyres to be placed under the tree.

Christmas Day this year was a curtailed gathering, due to the government's last-minute restrictions on households mingling, announced days before in an effort to restrict the bounce-back of covid. But as we awoke at my in-laws' house on Christmas morning, there was an excitement rarely felt as a fully grown adult. This year, the tree was less about baubles and more about the bounty of triathlon gear that lay beneath it, gifts that would fuel my Ironman aspirations!

Among the carefully curated collection of gifts, one parcel stood out with the smugness of a cat who's caught the canary. Briony had outdone herself, placing it front and centre like the star atop the tree. It was a soft, suspiciously large and shapely package that beckoned me with the promise of something a little special, and Briony was very giggly as she passed me the immaculately wrapped gift. Just like a child at Christmas, I ripped back the wrapping paper with the finesse of a raccoon getting into a bin bag.

And there it was – a wetsuit that was the stuff of Ironman legends, its neoprene gleaming like the Christmas star that guided wise men. It was a suit designed not just to swim in but to soar through the waves, a hydrodynamic marvel that whispered of personal bests and the sweet, sweet taste of transition-zone triumph. Okay, so it unfortunately had found an owner that hoped to just complete rather than compete in the Ironman, but for me it was everything I could have asked for.

I held it up to the light, half expecting a choir of angels to burst forth in song at the sight. It promised buoyancy that would make a cork look like an anchor and a fit that suggested it had been tailored by aquatic elves. This could be my secret weapon to duck under the dreaded 2 hour 20 minute cut-off in the swim section of the Ironman.

With each panel and seam, I could feel the culmination of countless hours of research, the designers' sleepless nights spent in pursuit of the ultimate swim experience. It boasted technology that I was sure could bend the laws of physics, a neoprene concoction spun from the same dreams that had inspired the Ironman challenge itself.

I slipped an arm through a sleeve. It was a perfect fit, a match made in triathlon heaven, and as I zipped it up I transformed not into a superhero, but a super-swimmer. In my mind's eye, I was already slicing through the water of Pennington Flash on race day, each stroke a testament to the genius of the suit's design.

Briony watched with a mixture of pride and bemusement as I paraded around the living room, practising my best streamline position. The Christmas tree seemed to nod in approval, its lights twinkling in what I assumed was admiration.

And so, as the last of the wrapping paper was cleared away and the remnants of our festive lunch were consigned to the history books, I sat, the proud owner of a new aquatic ally, ready to take on the lakes and oceans that stood between me and my Ironman dream. The wetsuit, now resting in its place of honour, was not just a garment, it was a mantle of responsibility, a neoprene promise that I was going to give this my all.

As the day wore on, the feast of turkey, trimmings and chocolates was a mere speed bump in my training regimen, the wetsuit a constant reminder that the waters of Ironman UK awaited. Briony, ever-supportive, watched with a mix of amusement and pride as I expressed more excitement for the snug fit of the wetsuit than the Christmas pudding and desserts on offer.

New Year's Eve was a much quieter affair than usual for everyone that year. The streets, the pubs, the city centres silent as the world awaited the birth of a new year. As 2020 had been a challenge for so many reasons, we all beckoned in a fresh start in 2021 more eagerly than most years. We all prayed Covid was behind us, that a return to some sort of normality would follow and, for me, of course Ironman. The customary clinking of glasses was replaced by the buzzing of phones, WhatsApp messages lighting up the night. A 'Well done on this week' from Coach Garrie pinged in, his message short but packed with the pride of a commander whose soldier was performing admirably on the front line.

Max and I swapped virtual words of encouragement, our digital celebration a testament to the camaraderie that had bloomed in the oddest of years. We wished one another a good year, with the promise of the famous red carpet leading to an Ironman finishing line in Bolton.

As the clock ticked towards midnight, I sat, not with a glass of champagne, but with a herbal tea. After all, there was an 8am run with my name on it. The Ironman journey had turned the festive season into an athlete's advent, where each day brought me closer to the goal I had once deemed as distant as the North Star.

My commitment, sealed by the routines of December and the promise encased in neoprene, was stronger than ever. The Ironman dream was no longer a distant echo but a roaring call to arms. And as I hit 'reply' to Coach Garrie's message, I knew that the true countdown had begun. The journey to Ironman UK was not just a possibility, it was a path I was already sprinting down, with the taste of energy gel on my tongue and the warmth of Briony's encouragement. Although, as we started 2021, there was also a thought that this was going to be an even bigger year of change than we had initially anticipated …

Chapter 14
The Bump in the Road

In a tale already crowded with sweat, gears and the relentless pursuit of Ironman glory, there came a subplot – one that, if I am honest, was much more important than wetsuits and bikes. This was one of hope, hormonal injections and the daunting world of IVF. Briony and I had embarked on a journey not around the triathlon course, but through the intricacies of fertility treatment. Unlike the Ironman journey that chronicles a year, this was at this point already a three-year marathon where at times we had been unsure whether a finishing line would ever be in sight and whether we'd get the chance to be parents.

One particular day stays long in the memory; after months of testing, we had been called in to receive the latest set of fertility results. The doctor, giving his best impression of a television quiz show host (think prime Les Dennis from *Family Fortunes*) read out our chances with a flourish. It was a bizarre mix of medical jargon and suspense, leaving us half expecting to be handed a consolation prize at the end. The doctor announced, 'We wanted to see this many eggs, your test results said … [insert dramatic pause]'. The upshot was, after two years, we were now deemed prime candidates for an NHS-backed attempt at IVF, all be it we were to be given just one shot.

We were on the NHS's starting blocks, awaiting our turn in the IVF relay. Then, as if on cue, Covid-19 entered stage left, throwing a spanner in the works with the finesse of a pantomime villain. Our NHS date was lost in a haze of lockdowns and uncertainty, leaving us with more questions than a toddler in the 'why' phase. After an already long wait, another frustrating period began. Our phone calls rang out unanswered, all communication ceased, and after eventually reaching someone after weeks of trying, we were encouraged to find a different route if we could possibly afford it. Any NHS support would be a long way off. A crushing blow after years of effort.

Unwilling to let our dreams be derailed by a virus that had already commandeered the global narrative, we turned to a private clinic. Google had once again been our friend and, after reading some very positive reviews, we made a virtual appointment with a clinic in Wilmslow. The decision came with the weight of financial consideration but carried the lightness of renewed hope. Think of what bike I could get instead? I am, of course, joking; some things you can't put a price on. December, typically a month of festivity and cheer, was repurposed into a regime not solely of training but now also of treatment, with me playing the dual role of supportive husband and amateur endocrinologist.

Briony faced the daily gauntlet of hormone injections with the unflinching resolve of a seasoned marathoner on her final push. I became the nervy and untrained wielder of the needles, with the pressure of knowing that, despite my lack of medical training, these injections were the bridge to our end goal.

Our December was devoid of the traditional countdown confections. Instead, our days were punctuated by the soft click of the syringe, the small hiss as the needle pierced the skin, and the quiet sigh of relief as each session concluded. This was our advent – a calendar of courage, where each day revealed not sweets but the sweet triumph of another day's medical treatment complete. That we were once again moving forward in our shared goal.

The steadfastness of Briony was a beacon that outshone any festive light display. With each passing day, as we navigated the peaks and troughs of hormone therapy, her resilience never wavered. She was the embodiment of the adage 'grace under pressure', her every action a testament to the depth of her resolve.

In the quiet of the night, post-injection, we'd sit wrapped in the comfort of each other's company, speaking in hushed tones of the future. Those moments became our sanctuary, a place where vulnerability and hope intertwined, strengthening the bond between us with the unspoken language of shared dreams.

As the month waned, and the final injection was administered, a sense of accomplishment enveloped us. We had weathered the storm together, each needle a lighthouse guiding us towards the shores of possibility. Briony's bravery, a constant through the tumult of hormones and uncertainty, was the undercurrent that propelled us forward.

As the new year rang in its infancy, we were ready. The clinic, with its sterile walls and compassionate smiles, became our coliseum. The fertilised egg, our beacon of potential, was carefully implanted. We knew the statistics were cold and clinical – a one-in-three shot at success even at this stage. However, with hope is a fire that statistics cannot quell. The process was over like a shot, and then began the waiting game: two weeks to find out if we were pregnant or not.

Mid-January brought with it the longest wait of our lives. Anticipation hung in the air, thick as the fog on a Manchester morning. The call from the doctor was to be our finish line, the culmination of years of hoping, trying and believing. We clung to every moment Briony felt something close to what could be considered morning sickness, yet refused at the same time to feel too excited without an official confirmation from the doctors.

Two weeks later, at a whistle-stop trip to the clinic, Briony's bloods were taken for testing, and then we were asked to go back home for the call that would determine whether we were pregnant or not. The phone rang, and for a moment we stood paralysed. I almost didn't want to answer; what if it was bad news and this was the end of the journey? The voice on the other end was calm, measured, yet within it carried the melody of our wildest dreams come true. It was confirmed. We were expecting a baby, due in October. The news washed over us like a wave over a weary swimmer, renewing our strength and bringing with it tears that were a cocktail of joy, relief and gratitude.

The road to Ironman, it seemed, was destined to be a dual carriageway, with two very distinct yet intertwined journeys. As I looked at Briony, I could see the genuine happiness in her eyes that she would become a mum. That was the moment that I knew our lives would be changing for ever.

It also reaffirmed that this really was my one last shot at Ironman, at least in the short term. Sleepless nights, parental responsibilities and play centres beckoned and, in the near term, that would not fuse well with the dedicated training and hours required for this monster triathlon.

'The Bump in the Road' was more than just a detour; it was a reward for our strength of partnership, and the sheer, unadulterated joy of life's unexpected victories. It was a reminder that the most challenging roads often lead to the most beautiful destinations. As we prepared for the arrival of our newest team member, I couldn't help but feel that this was the true victory lap. The Ironman would come and go, be what may in July 2021, but in October a whole different stage of life would begin.

Part 2: Training Breakdown

Chapter 15
The Digital Peloton –
A Journey in Messages

After the euphoria of needles, tests and baby talk had quietened down a little, it was back to my world of training, to refocus on the immediate task in hand. While Briony was eyeing up the latest running pram, cooing over baby grows and paint samples for our soon-to-be nursery, Coach Garrie reached out with an invitation. With my training due to step up (more on this shortly) I was asked if I wanted to join his merry band of athletes in his WhatsApp group. A mixture of people I was told, but containing a few fellow Ironman wannabes, some who would be there in Bolton. At first, I was unsure. This had always been a personal mission, and away from the interactions with fellow Ironman virgin Max, the journey had been me against me. Well, me against Coach Garrie's gruelling training programme. However, I had a sudden realisation that this mentality had not served me well last time. Lone wolf had not ultimately been healthy or successful and should not be my way forward this time around. The more I could surround myself with a digital support circle, surely it could only help my chances of running across July's finishing line in one piece. It was decided and I agreed that Coach Garrie would add me to his digital wolfpack.

Mid-January rolled in with the unceremonious arrival of a WhatsApp notification; it was time to introduce myself to Coach Garrie's inner circle. Suddenly, I was part of his digital peloton, a motley crew of athletes, bound not by proximity but by a shared passion for endurance sports and a tolerance for Coach Garrie's no-nonsense style.

It became clear shortly after, we had a wide range of characters, all with their own unique attributes and qualities.

The Tech Aficionados

This subgroup treated triathlon gear with the reverence of sacred artefacts. Their discussions about the latest GPS watches, heart-rate monitors and power meters were as detailed as an engineer's blueprint. Their daily debates – whether Garmin trumped Polar, or if the latest aero helmet could indeed shave seconds off a time trial – were as heated as a summit finish in the Tour de France. On the fence about a purchase? The Tech Afficionados were your go-to people.

The Marathon Devotees

These runners viewed 26.2 miles as a warm-up. Their weekly mileage updates were dizzying, their interval-training times enviable. In this group, tales of 'hitting the wall' were shared like war stories around a campfire, each recounting imbued with a mix of pride and masochistic pleasure. These were the folks who, upon hearing the word 'taper', would react as if you'd suggested they give up running for knitting. But if you were struggling with heart-rate thresholds and tempo runs, they were there in an instant to guide you through.

The Gear Gurus

Amidst our motley crew was this squadron of cycling savants whose knowledge of gear ratios and bike mechanics was so profound, I'd wager they could disassemble, grease and reassemble their bikes blindfolded (and I had a sneaky suspicion they did this at night). The Gear Gurus' discussions about derailleur adjustments and the merits of ceramic bearings were as intricate as a Swiss watchmaker's blueprints. They knew exactly what your set-up should be for your two-wheeled steed to navigate the hills of Bolton.

The Newcomers

These people were the beating heart of our WhatsApp peloton. Their journey was a live-action feed of athletic discovery. Every question posed, from the best type of running shoes to the intricacies of transition zones, was met with a flurry of responses. Their infectious enthusiasm reminded us all of the pure joy found in the early days of our sports journey. The Newcomers could often be spotted if a veteran of the group asked what bike they were training on, and they responded (like me) 'a silver one'. I was 100 per cent a signed-up member of this slightly naïve sub group.

The Iron Veterans

And then there were these grizzled warriors of triathlon, their skin weathered not just from age but from the sun, wind and the sheer grit of endurance racing. Their stories were a tapestry of triumphs, heartaches and wisdom, each anecdote a lesson in the art of perseverance. The vast majority were, thankfully, Ironman UK graduates, people who could relay every curve or bump in the Bolton roads.

The Group Cheerleaders

And, of course, the source of the positivity and the lifeblood of our little digital community were the Group Cheerleaders. Their unwavering positivity and good-natured banter was like a warm embrace on a cold morning. Whether celebrating a personal best or commiserating over a missed workout, their spirits never faded. They were the sunshine on our rainy training days, the enthusiastic fans on an otherwise desolate course. I was never sure whether they were actually training for an event themselves or just thrived off the successes of their digital brothers and sisters. Either way, they were always on hand with a positive meme or a virtual high-five on your latest training run.

The group chat buzzed from dawn till dusk. It was a virtual training camp, where encouragement was served for breakfast, advice for lunch and a hefty slice of humour for dinner.

Being early January, the Tech Aficionados were busy comparing the training gadgets they had received for Christmas. The Marathon Devotees, ever the overachievers, were still plotting out holiday-themed running routes, their Strava loops looking like misshapen reindeer.

The Newcomers, bless us, were all agog with the New Year spirit, and trepidation about the events that lay ahead. I was firmly in this camp. Their posts were filled with queries about the best sports-related gifts to pick up in the New Year sales, each suggestion eagerly noted down as if it were the secret to unlocking athletic potential.

The Iron Veterans, in their typical fashion, had announced their New Year race plans, and their New Year's resolutions were not mere statements but battle cries, each one a promise of pushing their limits further, of chasing down new challenges with the ferocity of a winter storm and setting new personal bests and qualifying times.

Our digital peloton was united. Training tips for the cold weather, strategies for balancing family and work with workouts, and motivational quotes flew back and forth. The group had become more than just a collection of athletes: it was a family, each member playing their part in keeping the spirit of endurance sports alive, even as the world outside remained in the grip of uncertainty.

Coach Garrie's messages, sometimes stern, often inspiring, always to the point, were the glue that held us together. His belief in our collective potential was the fire that kept us warm through the winter training months. He was the conductor and we were his sweaty, sweary, often fatigued orchestra.

We shared not just training plans but life's triumphs and tribulations, each message a thread in the fabric of our shared journey towards athletic and personal growth. Soon the group was filled with snowy scenes as the full force of the UK winter hit and derailed our long rides. It gave the Gear Gurus a chance to debate the best set-up for a snowy winter ride, while us Newcomers muted the group, retreated to our warm spare rooms and our ever-reliable turbo trainers.

As each of us pursued our individual goals, the group stood as a testament to the power of collective support. In a world turned upside down by a global pandemic and our ability to build new in-person relationships restricted, our digital peloton was a constant, a source of normality in a time of uncertainty. It was here, in this virtual gathering of like-minded souls, that the road to Ironman became a journey shared, a path walked – and ridden and swum – together. As the saying goes, 'If you want to go fast, go alone. If you want to go far, go together.'

Chapter 16

Building the Base – The January Chronicles

January 2021 arrived with the fanfare of a solo trumpet player in an empty stadium, heralding a month where my training schedule morphed from what felt like a friendly jog into a full-blown sprint, determined and unyielding. The gentle introduction from Coach Garrie was well and truly over. This was the month where 'Building the Base' transitioned from a catchy chapter title into a lived reality, a relentless pursuit of endurance, strength and the occasional bout of wondering, 'What on earth have I signed up for?' As Coach Garrie sent me my training plan for the next few weeks, I couldn't help but be unnerved by the heights that were expected of me; they seemed ambitious to the extreme.

My training diary, once a sparse landscape due largely to the closures and restrictions still in place in the UK, now brimmed with activity. Six days a week it beckoned with the sort of insistence usually reserved for a toddler demanding attention. Each day was a mosaic of running, cycling and longing glances at the pool – still off-limits due to the double whammy of winter chills and lockdown protocols.

The load was now hefty – a smorgasbord of seven to nine hours per week dedicated to turning myself into an Ironman-worthy machine. The cycling sessions were epics in their own right. Beyond the daily sprints and hill climbs, they began climaxing at 50-mile rides on the weekend, each journey a battle against what I'd previously deemed possible. But with every one, the 112-mile goal began to feel slowly more achievable.

Running wasn't left behind in this surge of activity. A couple of half-marathons were sprinkled into the mix, tossed in like casual afterthoughts by Coach Garrie, but in reality they were Herculean efforts that tested both my physical and mental mettle. Each step was a negotiation between my aspiring Ironman self and the part of me that still couldn't believe I was voluntarily doing this. The reality was these runs in isolation were feeling achievable, but how would I run double the distance after a mega swim and bike ride?

Then there was the fatigue – oh, the fatigue. It crept up like a ninja in fluffy slippers, subtle at first, then all-encompassing. It was a tiredness that really seeped into my bones. A little ever-present reminder of the load I was subjecting my body to. This wasn't the 'I stayed up too late watching Netflix' kind of tired. This was a deep, cellular exhaustion, the kind that made a flight of stairs look like Mount Everest. Although one could argue that this was perfect preparation for a new father ahead of welcoming a baby into the world!

Balancing this new training regime with work and home life was akin to juggling flaming torches while riding a unicycle. Each day was a tightrope walk of time management, where every minute counted and every missed training session felt like a personal defeat. I turned to the only man who would understand this pain: Max.

'How has the training been going so far?' I enquired. 'Just another set of intervals, but man I am feeling it,' replied Max. I asked how he did it – being already a parent, a business owner and a fellow Ironman wannabe. Here I was struggling to keep all the plates spinning and yet he seemed to be doing this and more with ease. He reassured me that, like myself, he was struggling. However, his approach was ruthless and methodical, each task faced with the same focus and determination he applied to his training. He compartmentalised his life in a way that made sense – Max knew his time was sacred, work was a necessary challenge, and training was his sanctuary.

In our exchanges, he shared tips on integrating workouts into a packed day, his non-negotiables, but also the sacrifices he was willing to make in the short term. He talked about the importance of quality over quantity in every training session: a philosophy that resonated with me and luckily my own Coach Garrie, as we sought to maximise the impact of each session. But beyond that he talked about the importance of being present not just in training but at home when it mattered.

Watching Max seamlessly blend his roles as a parent, professional and athlete was inspiring. It was a reminder that pursuing a goal as colossal as the Ironman didn't mean sacrificing every other aspect of your life; it was about integrating them, finding harmony in the chaos. Also at the same time, it was a recognition that giving 100 per cent to every aspect of our lives would not be possible in the short term; it was about picking your wins over the next few months.

As I moved through January, the image of Max, managing to keep all his plates spinning, often came to mind. It was a motivator, a beacon guiding me through the early mornings, the late-night workouts and the never-ending juggle of responsibilities. I was determined not to drop my own plates.

It gave me new-found focus to be there in both body and mind at home. The commitment to be present when paint colours for nurseries were discussed, to share the enjoyment of the baby bears sent in the post by family members and to make sure I realised that there was a much more important journey that needed my attention. I could not allow Ironman to engulf every aspect of my life.

As the weeks passed, something miraculous happened – adaptation. My body, initially shocked and indignant at the demands placed upon it, began to evolve. Muscles toughened, endurance grew and what once seemed impossible started to feel almost routine. The mind, too, adapted. The mental battles of dragging myself out of bed for a frosty morning ride became less about internal conflict and more about acknowledging the challenge and embracing it. The brain fog that flooded me in those morning meetings began to lift and clear.

The home front turned into a support station – Briony, ever the pillar of strength, provided encouragement and understanding, despite the occasional raised eyebrow at my increasingly bizarre eating habits (carb-loading doesn't always look pretty). As I discussed my fears of dropping one of the theoretical plates, a promise was made. Right now, sacrifices would have to be made and my training would remain high on my list of priorities right up until race day on 4 July. But no matter what the outcome was in the race – be it an Ironman medal or a big fat DNS stamped across my name – I'd be there in body and mind for the final few months before baby's arrival.

As the snow began to melt away, and the month drew to a close, I took a moment to acknowledge how far I'd come. The journey from hospital bed to lockdown jogger and now a six-day-a-week training machine was as much a surprise to me as it was to anyone who knew me. The half-marathons and lengthy bike rides, once daunting prospects, were now badges of honour, testaments to my growing capacity for endurance. The days in the hospital bed seemed a very distant memory.

The absence of swimming was a niggle, a gap in my triathlon armour that gnawed at me. What use was being bike- and marathon-ready if I didn't make the dreaded swimming cut-off? No matter, for now it was about controlling the controllable and British water temperatures and government guidelines were far outside of my control. Swimming would have to be for another day.

As I looked back in the pages of my training diary, January 2021 stood as a testament to growth, a chapter of transformation. This month hadn't just been about increased endurance and physical work. It had reset my boundaries and internal mindset. The road to Ironman UK was becoming less of a distant dream and more of a tangible, sweat-stained reality. The mileage that would be needed on 4 July suddenly looking within reach.

As I turned the calendar page to February, I did so with a sense of accomplishment and anticipation. The base was built, the groundwork laid. Going forward, it was time to build upon it, push further, faster and with more determination than ever. The Ironman quest was in full swing, and I was riding the wave, fatigued but unbroken, ready for whatever challenges lay ahead.

Chapter 17

The Real Road - A Spin on the Ironman Course

This chapter of my Ironman journey began with an open invitation from Coach Garrie's WhatsApp group. A chance to ride a lap of the actual Bolton Ironman bike course with a few other riders. As lockdown restrictions again started to ease, an outdoor, socially distanced ride was on offer. The snow and ice of the previous weeks had all but melted away, so there was little excuse not to join up. Still a mix of excitement and nerves wrestled within me as I contemplated the idea. The bulk of my riding so far had been confined to my indoor turbo trainer, a solo adventure. Now, here was a chance to see how I would fare in the real world and under the watchful eyes of others. However, this Ironman challenge was all about pushing my boundaries and taking me out of my comfort zone.

Agreeing to join them that next Sunday, I found myself one crisp morning pulling into a pub car park, the starting line of our mini adventure. The act of putting names to faces, previously just digital apparitions on my phone screen, was oddly thrilling. Slightly unnervingly I was one of very few newbies and was surrounded by some real characters whose training rides were already the stuff of legend, Bolton Ironman veterans with tales as tall as the hills we'd climb. Even a Kona Ironman Age Group qualifier was there. And, of course, Coach Garrie, our North Star was present, to guide the group.

The camaraderie was palpable as we set off, a peloton of mixed ambitions and abilities. Yet, barely into the first mile my nerves seemed to get the better of me. A fumbled gear change as we approached our first hill ascent sent my chain clattering off, a mechanical faux pas that had me cursing under my breath. The group, a little way up the hill, graciously paused as I wrestled with my bike; a tangle of loose greasy chains and reddening cheeks outwardly showed my levels of embarrassment as the incident confirmed my place as the group newbie.

With a slightly bruised ego, I followed the group up the first hill. After the false start, we embarked on the true test – the Bolton Ironman bike course. The route was a tapestry of Lancashire's finest landscapes, a mix of pastoral beauty and urban grit. The hills, though, were the real stars of the show. Each ascent was a battle, a gruelling push against gravity that had my legs screaming a chorus of protest.

As we cycled, the course unfolded its challenges – sharp turns, sneaky inclines, and descents that were equal parts exhilarating and terrifying. I clung on to the group, my determination fuelled by a mix of pride and the fear of being left behind. The veterans tackled the course with a familiarity born of many such rides, their ease both awe-inspiring and slightly demoralising as they casually held conversations, while I panted behind them.

Then, there was Garrie, who, sensing my struggle, dropped back to ride alongside me. His presence was both comforting and motivating. His words, a mix of encouragement and tough love, pushed me onward. 'You've got this,' he'd say, a mantra that became my mental fuel as we pushed towards the top of the third and final major incline.

As we neared the end of the loop, the realisation of what lay ahead hit me like a headwind. This course, with its relentless hills and deceptive stretches, was to be completed not once, but thrice come race day. The indoor training sessions, while valuable, suddenly seemed like child's play compared to the raw, unfiltered challenge of the actual course itself. This route was so much more challenging than my virtual world. The technique and mental concentration needed to weave through the tight corners and avoid the famed Bolton potholes was more of a drain than I had anticipated.

We finished the loop with a general sense of accomplishment, tinged with the sobering knowledge of the task ahead. Goodbyes were exchanged in the pub car park, for some this was a leisurely ride akin to a rest day for their experienced Ironman bodies. For me it was an education and a sobering serving of reality. As I drove home, the bike course replayed in my mind, each hill a reminder of the journey ahead.

That day's ride was more than a training session. It peeled back the layers of my training, revealing both the progress made and the mountains still to climb – both literal and metaphorical.

On arriving back at home, as I unloaded my bike from the back of my car, the weight of the Ironman challenge settled on my shoulders like a mantle. The road to Bolton, once an abstract concept navigated through virtual and indoor training, had taken on a new, tangible form. It was no longer just a course on a map or a segment on a training app; it was real, daunting and waiting.

In the quiet of the evening, as I sat nursing tired muscles and a new-found respect for the course, I realised that this was what Ironman training was truly about. It was about confronting the reality of the challenge, about stepping out of the comfort of controlled environments, and facing the unyielding truth of the road. This was never designed to be easy, and this time I was not alone. I reached out to the one man who would give me his years of wisdom and spare no feelings. Coach Garrie.

'I thought I'd hear from you,' Coach Garrie began, his tone a blend of mentorship and mild mischief. I was ready to unload my insecurities about the ride, the hills that felt like mountains and my place amidst the peloton of varying abilities. Before I could start Coach Garrie jumped in. 'You did fine out there. More than fine, actually,' he said, cutting through my self-doubt.

I raised an eyebrow, scepticism written across my face (not that he could see!) but the pregnant pause was enough for Coach Garrie to pick up on my suspicions. He chuckled, knowingly. 'Listen, this Bolton course is a beast. It chews you up and spits out the best of riders. But you – you hung on; you pushed through. That's what this is about.'

His words were soothing to the sting of my perceived inadequacies. 'But the hills, Garrie,' I protested, 'they were relentless. And my gear mishap …' Coach Garrie waved off my concerns. 'Hills are just nature's way of making you stronger. And as for the gear slip – happens to the best of us. It's how you recover that counts. You didn't let it beat you. That's the right spirit; you'll need that mentality come the big day.'

His reassurance was grounding, a reminder of the journey's purpose. 'It's all building blocks, you know,' he continued. 'Every ride, every hill, every little "mishap" – they're all pieces of the puzzle. You're getting stronger, more resilient. That's what matters. Let's remember, it's February, we still have four months of training to get you there.' I absorbed his words. Coach Garrie's ability to distil wisdom into a few sentences was akin to a chef turning simple ingredients into a gourmet meal.

'Remember, this is a marathon, not a sprint – figuratively speaking,' he added with a grin. 'You're laying down the foundation, brick by brick. Come race day, you'll be ready. Trust the process. Trust yourself.'

The conversation shifted then, from my performance to general training chatter – nutrition tips, recovery tricks, and the importance of mental fortitude. He then spared no feelings as he announced, 'Your bike set-up was terrible mind. What were you thinking with that massive water bottle on your front bars? Think about all that extra weight you were carrying.' He was right; it had seemed like a great idea to have a huge water bottle lodged at the front of the bike, between two newly attached tribars I'd fitted to the Boardman, despite never using them once during the lap. Right there, this conversation had given me a marginal gain, a small executional win, beyond the mental lift. The next day the tribars and the top-heavy water bottle were binned, never to be seen again.

Some late-night web surfing (not that kind) after my call with Coach Garrie formed the final part of my new plan. While Zwift training had been a key cornerstone in my initial training block, and would continue to be my midweek training partner, at weekends I would go another (virtual) route.

Enter Rovvy.com, an alternative training programme where I could virtually ride the dreaded Ironman loop from the comfort of my own home. Now there was no escaping those torrid hills whether I liked it or not. I vowed to switch it up weekly from now on in. Now the weather was clearer and the days were brighter, one weekend would be the torrid virtual hills of Bolton, next would be the local roads of Manchester, in an effort to improve my cycling technique out there in the real world.

As I dragged my sore legs to bed that night, I reflected on what had been one of the most pivotal moments in my Ironman story so far. It was a convergence of the virtual and the real world, and the intricate details were different between the two. A testament to the power of community, I had attempted and been humbled by the majesty of the mighty Ironman course. As I drifted off to sleep that night, the hills of Bolton lingered in my dreams, a constant, looming presence on the horizon of my aspirations.

Chapter 18
February's Forge – The Ebb and Flow

In the wake of my revelatory ride with Coach Garrie and his merry band of cyclists, February dawned with the promise of new challenges and a necessary pause. The first week post-ride was designated as my rest and recovery week, a period less about slackening the reins and more about giving my body the grace to absorb the rigours of January's relentless training.

This rest week was an exercise in restraint, a dance of low-intensity sessions designed to rejuvenate rather than exhaust. Six days were filled with gentle rides and easy jogs, each workout a delicate ballet of keeping the body in motion while allowing it to heal. It was a paradox of sorts – staying active to recover – but in the tapestry of Ironman training, it was a vital thread.

This week also afforded me the luxury of time that had been so absent in the previous few months. Time to catch up on the other facets of life that often played second fiddle to training. I found myself staying that extra hour or so in the office knowing the turbo trainer wasn't beckoning me that evening. Briony and I took to a leisurely walk at the weekend, embracing the crisp February air with the kind of appreciation that only comes after being sequestered in a cycle of intense training. Again, the chance to be present rather than always mentally plotting my next training session was a welcome relief.

But rest, like all good things, had to come to an end. Coach Garrie did not disappoint, as the final three weeks of February marked a return to the fray. The intensity of training ratcheted up once again, each week a careful orchestration of 9 to 11 hours' work, split between cycling and running. These were not just workouts; they were personal battles, each session a duel between my current limits and potential capabilities.

The roads of Cheshire became my proving grounds, the rolling hills a test of my burgeoning cycling prowess at the weekends. My running routes, a mix of urban sprints and pastoral jaunts, were trials by pavement, each mile a step closer to Ironman readiness.

As February waned, a new element was introduced to my training regimen – the brick session. To the uninitiated, a brick session might sound like a masonry workshop, but in triathlon vernacular, it's a back-to-back workout of biking followed by running. It's a dress rehearsal for the transition the body undergoes on race day, from pedalling powerhouse to fleet-footed runner.

The end of the month saw me embarking on my first brick session. I pitched up at my office car park in Alderley Edge and prepared for a feat that would combine a 53-mile cycle through the Cheshire countryside with a 30-minute run immediately after. The bike leg was a scenic tour of endurance, each pedal stroke a dialogue between me and the road, the countryside unfurling like a green tapestry as I aimed to maintain something akin to the speed that would be needed on the day. I balanced the speed of Wilmslow Bypass – long three-mile stretches where I could gather some speed – with the combination of nearby choppy hills, cutting through Holmes Chapel and Macclesfield to replicate some of the dreaded inclines that Bolton would deliver.

Upon completing the cycle, I arrived back at my parked car in Alderley Edge. The transition was swift – bike thrown in the back of the car, helmet off, running shoes laced. I grabbed an energy gel, a swig of electrolytes and away I stumbled. The switch from cycling to running was jarring, my legs initially protesting the change in motion. They were heavy, like lead, unsure of their new roles as I wobbled out of the car park and into the nearby woodlands on a path leading through the trees.

But as I settled into the run, the heaviness gave way to a rhythm, the initial awkwardness transforming into a steady stride. The 30 minutes of running post-cycle was a revelation, an insight into the unique demands of triathlon. It was training not just the body, but also the mind to adapt, to switch gears, and to persist when things felt tough. But with the amazing forest of Alderley Park surrounding me, there was a calm in the air, which at least did its best to soothe the soul if not the body.

I arrived back at my car, my bike abandoned on the lowered back seats, feeling good. The week's rest had done wonders for my recovery both physically and mentally. While I was tired from that back-to-back session, I felt like I still had some energy left in the tank. I was partly tempted to push on and do a little bit more, try to discover where my red line sat and what my body was now capable of, but I reminded myself to stick to Coach Garrie's plan. The 112-mile bike ride and a marathon, while still mammoth, was starting to feel somewhat achievable. Up until this point I had thrown myself with gusto at the bike and the run training and I was starting to feel the rewards. However, the lack of swimming opportunities was still nagging at me.

On 22 February 2021, a beacon of hope flickered through the long winter of restrictions. The UK government announced that there was to be a gradual easing of lockdown measures. This news arrived like the first warm breeze of spring, hinting at brighter days ahead, not just for the weary population but for triathletes like myself, thirsting for the return to open waters and the sanctity of swimming pools.

The promise of March was not just about the reawakening of nature but the resurgence of our training opportunities. The thought of diving into open water, which had been off-limits but now beckoned with its vast, open expanse, was both intimidating but welcome, as it was much needed.

Similarly, the reopening of swimming pools was like a reunion with an old friend from my previous training attempts. Pools were not just facilities; they were our training sanctuaries and one I definitely needed, in order to hone any swimming skills ahead of my 4 July date with the Ironman's 2.4-mile swim course.

The news was more than just a lifting of restrictions; it was a lifting of spirits. It reignited a sense of normality that had been dulled by months of uncertainty and adaptation. The final missing part of the puzzle, the swim. I could now plot a way forward.

As I marked the calendar, counting down the days to easing in March, the prospect of returning to open-water swimming and pool training filled me with a renewed sense of purpose. It was an opportunity to test the waters, quite literally, to gauge the progress in my endurance made during the countless hours on the turbo trainer and the treadmill. The reality was though, that it would leave me just four short months to layer on the technique required if I was to stand any chance of making that swim cut-off. This really was a race against time. If I couldn't make that 2 hour 20 minute cut-off on the swim, the officials would stop me before I got anywhere near the bike let alone my running trainers.

The easing of restrictions was also a reminder of the resilience of the human spirit. We had adapted, endured and found new ways to pursue our passions within the confines of a third lockdown at the most festive of times. I felt that through Coach Garrie, the new technologies such as turbo trainers and the little freedom we had been given, we had maximised our potential. Now was the time to master the third discipline.

Chapter 19

Diving into the Deep –
The Tim Ferris Philosophy

As the tides of my Ironman journey brought me to the shores of open-water swimming, it's time for a confession: while I meticulously followed Coach Garrie's cycling and running plans to the dot, my approach to swimming took a detour. Instead of swimming in Coach Garrie's lane, I found myself buoyed by the teachings of a different kind of guru – Tim Ferris.

For those unfamiliar with the world of personal self-optimisation, Ferris is something of a modern-day legend. The author of such works as *The 4-Hour Workweek*, Ferris is known for his ability to deconstruct complex skills and distil them into digestible, efficient learning strategies. His podcast, books and blog are akin to an Aladdin's cave of productivity and self-improvement treasures, attracting a global audience of eager learners and aspiring achievers.

But Ferris's influence extends beyond time management and entrepreneurship. His journey in mastering skills quickly led him into the realm of open-water swimming. Despite starting with a fear of water and barely being able to swim, Ferris applied his methodical approach to conquer his aquatic anxieties and became a proficient swimmer. His transformation was not just about fitness gains and hours in the pool, but more about mastering techniques and a testament to the power of a well-structured learning approach. His swimming technique, which he described in much detail on his Ted Talk, is called Total Immersion Swimming.

In my previous failed Ironman attempt, Ferris's philosophy had struck a chord with me. I became a believer, a disciple of his efficient, technique-driven approach to swimming. Buoyed by his success, I had booked eight lessons with a Total Immersion Swimming coach, embracing a methodology that promised not just to improve my swimming but to transform it.

Ah, Total Immersion Swimming – the Jedi training of the aquatic world. Total Immersion (TI) is less about thrashing your way to the other end of the pool and more about swimming smarter, not harder. It's all about streamlining your body, reducing drag, and making friends with the water rather than trying to conquer it with brute force.

The TI method teaches you to swim in a way that feels like you are part of the water, using techniques that are as fluid as they are effective. It's like learning a water-based ballet, where every movement is deliberate, every stroke purposeful. The result: you should depart the water with as much energy as you entered it, and given that I would face 112 miles on a bike and a marathon after that, you could see the appeal.

So, there I was, during that period in 2019, at the local swimming pool every Friday morning with my new swimming mentor. Week by week, my technique underwent a metamorphosis. Each lesson was a revelation, breaking down the complex mechanics of TI swimming into manageable, understandable components. My coach was part instructor, part aquatic alchemist, turning my clumsy splashes into a slightly more graceful – and crucially, efficient – stroke. From week one, when I could barely complete two lengths of the pool without gasping for air, and was being smugly beaten by the old ladies in the next lane, I was suddenly going back and forth with relative ease (and thankfully leaving the grannies behind me). My swimming didn't reach a particularly envious speed, but at least it contained a degree of efficiency that kept my energy levels on an even keel.

Then as you, dear reader, will know, my ego took over; cue the now well-told story. Overdoing the training, pushing my body to breaking point. Followed by cough, cough, cough – and into hospital this budding swimming legend went. The hours and cost of those swimming lessons as redundant as my Ironman 2019 race entry.

But 2021 would be different surely? Despite having gone two years with only the odd sporadic swim, I hoped that investment in the swimming lessons meant those skills would have stayed with me. So, I prepped myself for my first swim at the outdoor swimming facility at Media City.

Ah, open-water swimming in Media City – it's like taking a dip in the future! Imagine slipping into the water with the backdrop of high-tech studios and swanky offices, where the usual ducks and swans are replaced by the occasional drone buzzing overhead. The sleek, urban setting of Media City provides a unique twist to open-water swimming – you're half expecting a news anchor to narrate your strokes or a live broadcast of your freestyle technique. Each swim there feels a bit like you're starring in your own aquatic action movie, minus the dramatic soundtrack, but with all the adrenaline! Every Saturday morning, the locals would stare from their swanky Media City penthouses, sipping espressos as yours truly and equally madcap swimming voguers trundled down to the waterfront, wrapped in wetsuits, and dived into the chilled Salford Quays.

If you ever want to know what it feels like to be a human ice cube, try open-water swimming in Manchester in March. It's like Mother Nature decided to turn the water into her personal refrigerator. July's balmy 19°C waters of the Bolton Ironman seemed a distant dream as I faced the bone-chilling reality of early spring swimming in Manchester. At this time of year in Manchester's exposed waters, it's 5-10 °C. Let's just say, it was less 'refreshing dip' and more 'Arctic plunge'.

I had decided to invest in a trio of cold-water crusaders to help me with the lower temperatures: neoprene mittens, booties and an extra-thick neoprene swimming cap. These weren't just accessories; they were my lifelines, my defence against the icy clutches of hypothermia. The mittens and booties became my aquatic woolly socks and gloves, transforming my extremities from potential icicles into somewhat functioning limbs. Finally, the extra-thick neoprene cap. It wasn't quite like having a personal insulation system, but it did help turn what could have been a brain-freezing experience into a slightly more bearable encounter.

The plan, as foolhardy as it might have sounded to my shivering self, was to gradually wean off this protective gear over the coming months, as it would not be allowed for the Ironman race itself. But, for now, these items were essential as I entered the frigid waters. Let's see how much of my beloved Tim Ferris-driven form had carried over in the years that had passed.

Picture this: there I was, suited up in my neoprene armour, standing at the edge of the water in Media City, the urban landscape providing a stark contrast to the natural challenge ahead. The moment of truth arrived as I plunged in, ready to showcase my refined swimming technique. But as I submerged my head and prepared for that first, triumphant stroke, the cold hit me like a freight train made of ice cubes.

It was a shock so intense, so utterly bone-chilling, that every well-rehearsed plan and technique I had evaporated faster than morning mist. Fight or flight kicked in, and my body, in a state of icy panic, chose flight. I shot back to the surface, gasping for air, my initial poise reduced to a frantic, shivering doggy paddle.

Gone were the dreams of gliding through the water like a sleek, aquatic creature. Instead, I found myself floundering in a desperate attempt to catch my breath, stay calm and, well, just keep moving. Each stroke was less about form and more about survival, as I battled not only the cold but also the blow to my pride.

I managed a single, laborious 500m loop of Salford Quays, my body struggling to adapt to the shock of the cold. By the time I emerged from the water, I was a drenched, shivering mess rather than the conquering triathlete I had envisioned. The cold had been an unrelenting adversary, turning my first open-water swim of the season into a humbling, teeth-chattering experience.

As I grabbed my fleecy hoodie, big hat and anything else I had to get me warm, and stood there, teeth chattering and body quivering, I realised this was much more than just a physical challenge; it was a mental one as well. As I slowly warmed up, the blueness leaving my lips, I tried to logically assess the situation. I had been so desperate to return to the water but, let's face it, it was way too early in the year to be in the open water. You could call it a baptism of fire if it wasn't the compete opposite end of the heat spectrum. I had survived 500m, around one-eighth of what I would have to achieve on the day, and my form had been quite literally frozen out in favour of a doggy paddle that allowed me to keep my head above the freezing water. But I had completed it in around 20 minutes, not too far off the equivalent of the cut-off time for Ironman. I needed to stay positive.

The journey to Ironman is often painted as a test of physical endurance, but my swimming saga reminded me that it's also a journey of learning, adaptation and mental fortitude. As I looked ahead to the rest of my training, I did so with a renewed sense of optimism, ready to dive into whatever challenges lay ahead, both in the water and beyond, I just hoped it would be a good few degrees warmer next time.

Chapter 20
The Fuelling Frenzy –
A Calorific Conundrum

As March drew to a close and my training intensified under Coach Garrie's rigorous regime, fatigue returned, becoming my uninvited houseguest. It lingered like a mental fog, a constant reminder of the escalating demands of Ironman training. Last time a rest week allowed me to reset, but now, with the Ironman just a little more than three months away, the chance to pull back on training wasn't really an option. The additional hours Coach Garrie prescribed were taking their toll, each session a draining duel between my aspirations and my energy reserves.

In my quest for endurance glory, I delved into the science of calorific expenditure. Swimming, cycling and running each devour calories at rates as voracious as my new-found hunger. I learned that an average hour of swimming could burn a whopping 700 calories, cycling could torch around 600 calories, and running could consume a staggering 900 calories an hour! These weren't just workouts; they were infernos of energy expenditure. Multiply that calorie deficit over the hours I was now clocking up, and I was burning anything up to 8,000 additional calories each week. Each morning greeted me with a weariness that clung to my bones. My routine had become a relentless loop of train, work, sleep, repeat. The novelty of being an Ironman-in-training had given way to the grind of reality. I was a hamster on a wheel, running ever faster but getting nowhere in terms of energy required, and my consumption of food had not adapted to the new strains I was putting on my body.

Then came the day of the bonk, the driver that solidified my decision that change was needed. For those unfamiliar, 'bonking' is not a slapstick comedy move or a dive in the sheets with your better half; it's a total collapse of energy levels, a sudden visit to the dreaded 'wall'. Midway through a ten-mile run, my energy levels plummeted, leaving me dizzy, disorientated and dragging myself home in a state that was part exhaustion, part existential crisis. There I was, shuffling through the door, a shadow of my usual sprightly training self, more zombie than athlete and looking grey. It was then that Briony witnessed the aftermath of my calorific crash. 'You look like you've seen a ghost,' she exclaimed, 'and are you shaking?'

Her words were spoken half in jest and half deadly serious and her care in that moment was a reminder of the support system I had in her. She helped me to the sofa, her actions speaking the universal language of comfort. As I sat there, sipping on a recovery drink and a herbal tea, Briony's presence was a quiet reassurance. Here she was, two months pregnant when I should be supporting her, and she was the one looking after me.

Again, this was a time for more experienced heads, the people I had chosen to surround myself with for this journey. I reached out to Max, the WhatsApp group, and Coach Garrie, my digital lifelines in this sea of fatigue. The consensus was clear – my nutrition was off-kilter. I was burning the candle at both ends, and anywhere else a candle could feasibly burn. The revelation was simple yet profound – I needed to eat more. My body was a car, and like any car it required fuel to function. I was refusing to take my foot off the accelerator while ignoring every petrol station in sight. The rigours of Ironman training demanded a calorie intake that was beyond my usual diet. It was about feeding the beast within, providing it with the sustenance needed to swim, bike and run.

During exercise though, it became a little more complex. I needed to find a way to get enough calories in my body to face anywhere between 14 to 17 hours in constant motion on race day. Thus began my foray into the world of sports nutrition, a landscape dotted with everything from beef jerky to caffeine-laden gummies. Each snack promised the energy of a thousand suns but often delivered the digestive tranquillity of a turbulent sea. I became a culinary explorer, charting a course through a sea of protein bars, energy drinks and gels.

Amidst my grand experiment with sports nutrition, there came the chapter of caffeine gummies. Ah, these gummies! They appeared innocent, like colourful, sugary treats from a pick-n-mix. The allure was undeniable – who wouldn't want their energy fix packaged in a sweet, chewable, gummy form? So, with the enthusiasm of a kid in a sweet shop, I pocketed a few before a long Sunday morning run, expecting a burst of caffeinated vigour. Five miles in, I popped the first of them, and waited for the rush.

However, barely five minutes later a rumble of dissent echoed through my stomach. It wasn't the powerful surge of energy I had anticipated, but a more urgent, less welcome kind of surge. I quickly realised these gummy bears were more like grizzly bears, stirring a rebellion in my digestive system.

The situation escalated rapidly, and there I was, miles from home, in the grips of a caffeine-induced gastrointestinal tempest. Salvation came in the form of a timely located McDonald's, its golden arches a beacon of hope in my moment of distress. I dashed into the bathroom, ignoring the stares of the blurry eyed servers and early morning gatherers. In doing so, I narrowly avoided a 'Paula' and what would have certainly been a low point in this Ironman adventure.

This escapade with caffeine gummies was a stark, somewhat uncomfortable reminder that not all energy supplements are created equal. While the child in me rejoiced at the candy-like energy source, my adult self learned a valuable lesson about reading labels and respecting the potent effects of caffeine on the body. It was a humbling experience, one that added a comical yet cautionary tale to my journey of nutritional discovery.

My salvation came in the form of carb-fuelled sports powder, which, when mixed with water, became less of a beverage and more a lifeline. 'Tailwind' was a blend of calories, electrolytes and hydration, a trifecta of fuelling that was easy on the stomach and even easier on the taste buds. Designed to be consumed on the bike, it was a liquid companion to keep the bonk at bay. It kept my hands free, and, with a cola flavour, seemed to keep me topped up and focused. Plus, I could scoop directly into my newly purchased Coach Garrie-approved water bottles, mounted to my bike. It was a relief to finally find a solution that seemed to be easy on the stomach and kept my energy levels on the straight and narrow.

For the run, after many trial-and-error tests, Maurten gels became my go-to. These weren't your average gels; they were a sophisticated cocktail of carbohydrates, encapsulated in a hydrogel designed for efficient energy delivery. While a little tasteless, they settled well on the stomach (no repeat of the caffeine gummy incident) and kept the shaking, jittery bonk away. It helped that they were the Ironman official sponsor this year, so they would be readily available on the course come race day.

As I adjusted my diet, the change was palpable. My energy levels began to rise from the ashes of exhaustion. The morning weariness receded, replaced by a renewed vigour. The bonking became a distant memory, but a cautionary tale of what happens when nutrition takes a back seat in endurance training. The gels and carbohydrate mix kept me on better form in my sessions.

This chapter of my Ironman journey was a lesson in the importance of fuelling. This wasn't a race to turn up and power through. Half of it would be fought in the kitchen and at the dining table. Tailwind and Maurten became more than products; they were integral parts of my training arsenal. No scrimping any more on the fuel; they were to be as important as my running shoes and the bike.

That week I realised that becoming an Ironman is not just about physical training. I had to understand and respect my body's increased needs as I demanded more from it. It's a dance of calories and exertion, a balancing act that is as crucial as any swim stroke, pedal push or stride. In the world of triathlon, the right fuel is just as important as the right gear, and in this chapter I learned to fuel not just for the finish line, but for the journey itself.

Chapter 21

Marching Onward – A Symphony of Splash, Pedal and Run

March's training chapter was a tale of ups and downs, filled with periods of improvement, the occasional stumble and heaps of learning. It was a month where every stroke, pedal and stride were a note in the grand symphony of my Ironman preparation.

March arrived with a promise of longer days and even longer training sessions. As the calendar pages flipped, so did the intensity and volume of Coach Garrie's workouts. The month became a grand crescendo in my Ironman symphony, peaking at a staggering 13 hours per week.

The increase wasn't just felt in the ticking clock; it was measured in the miles under my belt, the litres of sweat I lost and the mountains of laundry that seemed to multiply like enthusiastic rabbits who had the right idea about what a bonk was.

As the hours intensified, so did my relationship with training. It was no longer a mere activity but a lifestyle choice, a daily ritual as ingrained as my morning cup of coffee (which, incidentally, became a non-negotiable necessity).

In the glass-half-full view, this month heralded a welcome return to outdoor swimming, a transition that felt both exhilarating and daunting. As I recalled slicing through (well … doggy-paddling) the waters of Media City, I was filled with mixed emotions. The donning of the wetsuit, the swim cap, the goggles, the feeling of open water around me took me mentally closer to the Ironman swim. Yet, with this new-found freedom came the realisation of the mammoth task ahead. Each stroke in the chilly waters was a question posed, and while I had three months for the water to heat up a few degrees, the reality was the work would need to be done to get me to an Ironman-worthy condition. The glass-half-empty part of me doubted whether I would truly be Ironman-ready. Would I be capable of achieving this required distance away from the warmth of a heated pool, and perform surrounded by the unique conditions of Bolton's Pennington Flash?

On the cycling front, confidence was blooming like springtime daffodils. The long weekend rides out on the rolling plains of Cheshire became my battleground, where I tested my endurance and mettle every other Sunday. Each journey was a blend of grit, scenic views and the occasional roadside snack. These rides were more than training; they were adventures on two wheels, each mile a story, each hill a chapter in itself. After the confines of a year in lockdown, it was exhilarating discovering all the nearby towns and villages that had passed me by when longer travel had been on offer. It was strange and a wake-up call to the beauty of the local landscape that I'd left undiscovered as we'd so often raced to the airport for city breaks overseas.

Then came the virtual world of Rouvy, a digital realm where I honed my skills and familiarity with the Bolton Ironman course. Rouvy was not any better than the much preferred and popular Zwift, still a mainstay in my mid-week turbo challenges set by Coach Garrie. What this training tool gave me was a confidence boost. It allowed me to jump on the bike and pedal the Ironman course's twists, turns and gradients, all from the comfort of home, the screen in front of me literally displaying a dreary Bolton skyline as I clocked up the miles. This blend of real-world rides and virtual training crafted a cyclist more prepared, more aware and decidedly more ready for the challenges of Ironman. From the previous month's nervous loop, where I had felt out of my depth, suddenly I was progressing past completing a solo loop, and was now capable of hitting two laps of the Ironman course.

Nutrition, my once Achilles' heel, had become a source of strength. Understanding the calorific demands of my training regime was like finding the missing piece of a puzzle. This meant not only was I feeling more comfortable with my hectic training schedule, but my performance and concentration at work were enhanced too. Every meal, snack and supplement fuelled my body for the rigours of training. I cannot pretend it was an exact science, but the loosening of the calorie restrictions was helping; peanut butter and jam bagels, alongside dark chocolate and peanut butter porridge became my calorific friends. The race nutrition, with Tailwind on the bike and Maurten gels on the run, was working wonders. No longer was I a hapless experimenter; I had a strategy, and my performance was paying dividends.

The introduction of brick sessions was a game-changer, again more so for my mental road map of progression. Transitioning from bike to run, my legs learned the art of switching disciplines seamlessly. Initially, these sessions were a jolt to the system – my legs felt like jelly, unsure of whether to spin or stride. But with practice, this uneasiness gave way to fluidity. The brick sessions were more than physical workouts; they were mental rehearsals, teaching my body and mind the nuances of transitioning from one discipline to the next that would be so needed for Ironman, especially if I was getting a little too close to those dreaded cut-offs.

In the midst of this escalating training saga, Coach Garrie chimed in, a monthly catch-up in our diaries, his message popping up like a beacon of wisdom in a sea of sweat and gears. 'You're doing brilliantly,' he began, his words a virtual pat on the back. 'But,' – and there's always a 'but' with Coach Garrie, like a plot twist in a thriller novel

– 'with three months to go, we need to dive deeper into your swim training. It's time to make waves.' Literally, I thought.

Of course, Coach Garrie was right. The swim leg was my Achilles heel, the part of the triathlon that lingered in the back of my mind like an unfinished chapter and still had the potential to derail all this hard work.

Coach Garrie also addressed the elephant in the room – my recent fatigue concerns. 'That bonk was a warning shot,' he said, mixing concern with his trademark no-nonsense approach. 'It's a sign we need to take a moment, recalibrate and adjust. Let's start next month with a week of rest and recovery. We'll dial it back to five hours, give your body a chance to catch its breath.'

Ah, rest and recovery – music to my ears … and to my aching muscles. Coach Garrie's plan was like a welcome plot twist in my training narrative, a necessary pause in the midst of the action. It was a pertinent reminder that sometimes, to move forward, you need to step back and gather the strength needed for the next chapter in the journey.

This message from Coach Garrie was more than just a training update; it was a strategic pivot, a recalibration of my journey. It underscored the importance of balance – the delicate dance between pushing hard and pulling back. As I absorbed his words, I remembered last time, the exhaustion and the illness that had put me in the hospital bed. The prospect of a lighter week was a slight relief, a reminder of how crucial and valuable it was to have an experienced head like Coach Garrie in my corner. Plus, there was a genuine excitement for the swim-focused chapter ahead. Next month's swimming adventures were to be framed as a new challenge, a new skill to master.

As March bowed out and April beckoned, I knew that the next phase of my Ironman preparation would be crucial. It was time to make peace with the water, to turn my weakest link into a strength or at the very least not a hindrance. With Coach Garrie's guidance and a week of recovery to recharge, I was ready for the next plunge – both into the pool when allowed, and into the final stretch of my Ironman training.

In this chapter of my Ironman saga, I had not only trained, I had transformed. Each day was a step closer to the ultimate goal, each challenge a lesson learned. The journey was shaping me, not just as an athlete but as an individual. I felt my mentality hardening, my belief growing. The symphony of splash, pedal and run was reaching a crescendo, and I was its conductor, ready to lead it to a triumphant finale.

Chapter 22
The Mind Games – Fortitude and Family

April arrived with a spring in its step, buoyed by me waking to a week-long lighter training schedule. It was a welcome break allowed by Coach Garrie, a much-needed respite in my Ironman journey. As I embraced this lull to a mere five hours of training per week, life outside the triathlon bubble was brewing with milestones and a virtual rendezvous which I could now focus on.

That week coincided with the most important event in mine and Briony's calendar, which eclipsed even the most gruelling of training sessions – our three-month baby scan. Briony and I, hand in hand, albeit a bit jittery, witnessed the miracle of our growing baby. The image on the screen was a beacon of joy, a tiny heartbeat drumming away, a rhythm of new beginnings. It was a profound moment, a blend of awe and relief, as we learned we had a healthy baby on the way. After a three-year journey to get to this moment, tears were shed, and fittingly a celebratory Nando's was shared (added calories were needed, right?). Sharing the news with friends and family, who had been distant due to restrictions, was amazing. Calls and messages buzzed with excitement and congratulations; we could now start planning as much as possible for the next stage, and Briony – free of the side effects of that first trimester – plotted the baby's arrival with an attention to detail that Coach Garrie would be proud of.

In the midst of this more restful week, I found time for a virtual catch-up with Max. Face-to-face meetings were still off the table under lockdown rules, but our digital connection bridged the gap. Max and I shared the highs and lows of our respective journeys, the triumphs and the tribulations, and contrasted the two equally gruesome plans passed on. These catch-ups with Max during this time were a pillar of support, a reminder that I wasn't alone in this endeavour. Our friendship, forged in the fires of shared challenges, had become a vital part of both of our training journeys. It reminded me how important it was in life in general to surround yourself with positive forces; they just seemed to make that journey that little bit smoother.

Across our Zoom meeting, we delved deeper into the different aspects of our Ironman journeys. It dawned on us that while the physical training was monumental, the mental fortitude required was colossal. Our conversation veered into the realm of mental conditioning, swapping book titles and podcast recommendations. We went beyond casual exchanges over our preferences for energy gels and running trainer choices; we shared mental ammunition, preparing us for the psychological marathon and potential torment we could face during the Ironman.

Our bedtime reading lists and audio books for long runs were transformed. Gone were the light-hearted novels and autobiographies of 90s footballers, replaced by podcasts and talks on mindset and endurance. We devoured stories of prolific triathletes and Ironmen, drawing inspiration and wisdom from their experiences. Chrissie Wellington's journey, in particular, resonated with me. Her underdog story showed mental tenacity, coupled with her athletic prowess, and painted a portrait of the kind of resilience we aspired to embody on our journeys. She had beaten the odds that were stacked against her.

Yet, amidst this library of inspiration, one figure stood out like a lighthouse in the stormy seas of endurance training – David Goggins. To call Goggins a mere athlete would be to call Everest a mere hill. Goggins is a force of nature, a man whose life story reads like an odyssey of willpower and grit. A retired Navy SEAL, ultra-endurance athlete and a former world record holder for the most pull-ups done in 24 hours, Goggins' journey is a testament to the power of the human spirit and made training for an Ironman look like child's play.

His first book, *Can't Hurt Me*, was less memoir and more a Haynes manual for mental toughness. Goggins doesn't just share his story; he throws down a gauntlet, challenging the reader to confront their own limits and push beyond them. His philosophy of 'embracing the suck', of turning obstacles into opportunities for growth, struck a chord with Max and me. Goggins was a man who had faced unimaginable hardships in his life, beyond anything I could comprehend. He emerged not just unscathed, but stronger, fiercer and more resilient.

Reading about Goggins' relentless pursuit of pushing beyond perceived boundaries, his unyielding discipline and his refusal to accept mediocrity, we both found a source of immense inspiration. His story was a beacon, guiding us through the mental fog that often accompanied rigorous training. Our discussions about Goggins and his extraordinary feats evolved into a deeper realisation about our Ironman journeys. We understood that while the physical aspect was critical, the battle was won or lost in the mind. Ironman was not just an endurance event, it was a mental crucible, forging a resilience that extended far beyond the race course.

As April marched on, armed with these new insights into mental fortitude, I found a renewed vigour for the training ahead. The physical workouts remained demanding, but mentally I was stronger, more focused. The stories of Wellington and Goggins, their triumphs and trials, became my mental fuel, igniting a fire of determination and perseverance.

This chapter of the journey was a revelation. It was a shift from viewing Ironman as a purely physical challenge to understanding it as a mental expedition. Every swim, bike and run so far had been classed as training the body.

Now, however, it was understood that these sessions shared a dual purpose; they were also key to the conditioning of the mind. There was the realisation that mental strength training would be just as crucial as the physical endurance during the next three-month period. That understanding was a turning point in this journey, a pivotal moment in my quest to become an Ironman.

I realised that while Ironman was a year-long quest, tagged with a definitive goal and finish line, what it was doing would potentially have a much more long-term impact. It was shaping me into a person who could withstand the rigours of life just that little bit better. I was becoming someone who could find the balance amidst the chaos and who could draw strength from the very act of pushing limits. This mental fortitude was perhaps the most valuable takeaway from my training – a gift that would continue to serve me long after the Ironman was over.

As that week of rest and recuperation drew to a close, I started to look forward to what the rest of April had in store for me, the body rested and ready to go. Coach Garrie's next few weeks had pinged into my inbox, and now I was ready with a new-found sense of anticipation. The journey so far had been tough, of that there was little doubt, and it showed no signs of slowing down until I crossed that start line in three months' time. This juggling of work, life and training; the hours needed to be found; the mental strength to go again when I was tired and could easily stay at home. This was not just about training for an event a few months away, I was training for that next stage of life. And as I had started the year celebrating that Briony and I would welcome a new life into the world, I now felt a sense of confidence and preparedness for everything beyond. The road to Ironman was tough, but it was preparing me for one of life's greatest adventures – parenthood.

Chapter 23
Wobbly Wheels and Life's Quirks

Just when I thought I had this Ironman training all figured out, with swimming finally looking up, cycling and running in a consistent groove and my mental fortitude seemingly unshakable thanks to my daily dose of Goggins, life decided to throw a spanner in the works. Welcome to the chapter I like to call 'Wobbly Wheels and Life's Quirks' – a week where my well-laid plans went as flat as a cheap bike tyre.

Let me set the scene: after a period of positivity and progress, life, in its infinite unpredictability, decided to remind me who's really in charge. Despite a restful week and an uptick in swimming prowess, the universe conspired to make fitting in training sessions as challenging as solving a Rubik's Cube blindfolded.

Now, I haven't delved much into my work life, but here's a brief summary: I work in ecommerce for a beauty brand, a sector that due to Covid, saw demand increase as everyone was forced indoors and beauty salons closed. It was seven days a week of digital madness – navigating the tumultuous waters of increased online shoppers and the never-ending saga of getting hold of stock for the business to meet that increased demand. It was an absolute roller coaster, and one that had required a healthy dose of dedication by me and my team to keep the wheels on. I had built up enough goodwill with my bosses over that period and the previous years to carve out time for training when needed – a lunch run here, an occasional quick pack-up-and-race-off at 5pm on the dot to get on the bike. The balancing act of work and training had been largely successful so far. Being still child-free for the next few months at least had meant I had kept both sides (and Briony) happy. But this week, work commitments piled up like a traffic jam on the M6.

Deadlines loomed like ominous clouds, and surprise meetings popped up, snatching away any hope of lunchtime runs. My days stretched longer than a weekend training session, each working day inching into the evening, taking the time earmarked for training. 'A few days,' I thought. 'I can just jiggle my days around this week.' Then one missed session became two, and the pattern continued.

In the midst of this work chaos, a personal curveball was thrown our way. Without delving into the nitty-gritty, Briony and I had a moment that sent our hearts racing – a common story for soon-to-be parents but nerve-wracking nonetheless. We booked a private scan for the very next day, needing that reassurance that everything was alright. Thankfully, it was, but that evening was anything but relaxing and nowhere close to being a situation where I could contemplate leaving Briony's side. An all too predictable restless, sleep-deprived night followed and the next day was no better, with the hospital scan scheduled for that evening, further eating into my training schedule. But seeing our little one healthy and active on the screen again was worth every missed mile and unattended workout. It was a moment of pure joy, a reminder of the bigger picture beyond swim-bike-run.

This week was anything but a masterclass in the art of juggling the unexpected. My Ironman journey, usually so regimented and predictable, was thrown into disarray by the demands of work, the responsibilities of being a good employee and the emotional roller coaster of impending parenthood. It was a stark reminder that training for an Ironman as a mere mortal doesn't happen in a vacuum – it's part of the larger, often messy, tapestry of life that placed other demands on my time, if I didn't quickly want to be divorced and jobless.

Towards the end of that chaotic week, my phone buzzed with an incoming call from Coach Garrie. I knew before answering what the topic of conversation would be – my training log was looking as barren as a desert. What had once been a sea of greens – a calling card that I had completed the session – was a collection of amber (indicating part-complete sessions) and, the worst part, a big red, indicating a missed session. I had completed the same total of training hours that week as I had in my previous rest week, a shortfall of around eight hours from what was planned. The call wasn't a surprise; Coach Garrie was dedicated to his athletes and had an eagle-eye for their training patterns, or in my case the sudden lack thereof.

As I answered, Coach Garrie's voice, ever the blend of sternness and support, filled the line. 'I've noticed a bit of a gap in your training log,' he began, his tone not *too* accusatory but observant. There was a pause, a silent acknowledgment of the hectic week I'd had. He didn't need to spell it out; he knew that life sometimes throws curveballs that even the best-laid training plans can't accommodate.

'You know, a one-off week is not going to derail your Ironman,' Coach Garrie continued, his words a relief to my frazzled nerves. 'I know, but we are on a ticking clock here. We can't afford too many of these,' I replied. His voice was the audio equivalent of a firm, guiding hand on my shoulder – reassuring yet urging me not to lose focus.

We talked through the week's events, and Coach Garrie listened, his responses a mix of empathy and pragmatism. He understood the delicate balancing act of training for an Ironman while navigating the demands of work and personal life. He explained I was not a pro athlete and neither were the others who he trained. However much we were dedicated to the plan, this could happen. As always, Coach Garrie was quick to remind me of the bigger picture. I felt the pressure on me ease just a little.

'This journey is as much mental as it is physical,' he said. 'Life's going to throw obstacles in your path, but it's how you navigate them that counts. Do not let a rough week throw you off course. Use it as fuel, learn from it and come back stronger.'

Despite the reassuring words, then came the closest thing he gave me to a warning; next week the real fun would begin, this phase of his plan was over and we'd be progressing to the next stage. With just about 11 weeks to go to race day, this would be the start of the peak training stage.

As the call ended, I felt a renewed sense of hope, exactly what was needed after what had been a particularly rubbish week all-round, Coach Garrie's words resonated with me, a reminder that the path to Ironman is never linear. It's filled with ups and downs, successes and setbacks. This bad week was just a small bump in the long journey I was on. One bad week wouldn't define my Ironman. However, my response to it potentially would. I could let this week knock me down, or I could shake off this setback, realign my focus and get back on the training track. With Coach Garrie's guidance, and a renewed resolve, I was ready to face the challenges ahead, one stroke, pedal and stride at a time.

The chapter of wobbly wheels was a humbling experience. It underscored the need for flexibility, for the ability to adapt and roll with life's punches. The week might have been a setback in terms of training hours, but it was a valuable lesson in perspective, patience and prioritisation.

This road to Ironman was proving to be as unpredictable as it was challenging. As soon as you felt you had it all figured out, there was another twist and turn. However, I was learning to adapt and not let every bump in the road (or wobbly wheel) derail my path. With that mindset and the week now behind me, I prepared to step back on to the training path, ready for whatever lay ahead, be it smooth roads or hidden tight corners.

Chapter 24
April's Athlete – Stepping Up the Game

After my rocky start to April, it was time to tackle the start of the peak training phase with gusto. Coach Garrie certainly wasn't lying: what was in front of me felt like less of a step up in the training plan, more a giant leap. The weeks ahead promised to be an all-out assault on my current physical and mental limits. But armed with determination and a poor seven days, I was ready to take on this beast.

The numbers themselves were daunting. The next week clocked in at a solid 13 hours of training, akin to my biggest week so far. Then came the behemoth – a gruelling 17-hour week that loomed over me like a mountain. Yet, with each day, each session, I chipped away at this mountain, turning what seemed impossible into the possible.

My weeks started to fall into a relentless yet rewarding rhythm. Monday to Friday, I became a master of the one-hour sessions. Whether this was an early morning dash to the pool, feeling my lungs burn on hill repeats on the turbo trainer, or pushing the pace on the pavement, each day was a focused burst of Ironman preparation. This was all about short intense sessions that carried the best bang for their buck.

Friday was earmarked for the long run. Now typically in the 15-mile range, this became the perfect excuse to run the 13-or-so miles from my home in Timperley to my office in Alderley Edge, adding a few detours to top up the total. These slow and steady runs became a great reflection point in my week, while I was mentally preparing myself for the weekend ahead. There was something quite satisfying, knowing that while most people had fought through early morning rush-hour traffic (by now most UK offices had people back in), I had donned the trainers and completed a half-marathon and then some before the working day had even begun.

Saturdays brought a change of scenery and a reintroduction to the open waters of Media City. This had quickly transformed from my absolutely worst workout of the week, a low point of my training at the start of the month, to one of my favourites. Despite being a little over three months pregnant, Briony continued to blow my mind, as she joined me on the drive every Saturday and would run laps of Salford Quays while I swam. It became our little joint adventure, and every once in a while, as I turned to breathe, I'd catch the mum-to-be scampering past me.

The cold, open water was no longer a fearsome adversary but a challenging friend. The hours I had spent that month in the pool, the one big positive, were starting to pay dividends. Each week the initial shock of the cold as it engulfed my wetsuit would still hit me. However, with every session, I was becoming calmer and more relaxed in the environment. My Tim-Ferris-inspired moves were slowly but surely transferring to the murkier and colder temperatures of open water. A surprising added benefit I was finding was the forced calm of open-water swimming. Unlike my day job, where I was a message away at all times, and my run and bike where my Garmin and bike computer would be constantly feeding me with information about speeds, distances and heart rates, this was stripped back. Here I was, out in the open water, unable to see more than a few feet in front of me. It forced me to be present, in almost a meditative way, alone with my thoughts. By the end of the month, I was comfortably clocking up 1,500m-plus in the water. Still not quite one third of my total, but a significant improvement on how I had started the month.

Then came Sundays – the crown jewel of Coach Garrie's training week. The initial panic of the Bolton Ironman course hadn't quite disappeared, but my hours riding the virtual version of the course had started to quell it to a more respectful rather than fearful mentality. The improved nutrition was certainly helping to even out my energy levels on the bike, and it led to two back-to-back weeks covering 65 miles each time, about the equivalent of two laps of the Ironman course. The second week even saw me dismount the bike and tag on a short run, to add a few more miles to my weekly total. Crucially at this point I was averaging a speed of around 15mph. Depending on how I performed on the day in the swim, and how quickly I progressed through transition, I would have at best around eight hours to complete the bike course. While that seems like a long time, factor in that those 112 miles would take me over significant climbs. The speed I was achieving was just about enough, but could I keep it up over the full distance?

At the end of that gruelling 17-hour week, the biggest commitment I had achieved in my training so far, I realised how needed this was. The crazy part was, with the race's 17-hour cut-off point, this was the first week I had achieved the cumulative distances that would be needed on the big day. It was a scary proposition to know I was two months away from needing to achieve this all in one go!

The month had certainly been a mixed bag. A rest week, followed by a week from hell had made April feel somewhat stop-start. On the positive side, while the increased training hours in the last two weeks had been tough, there was no doubt about it, they had brought with them a sense of accomplishment that was much needed. A mental win. The swim training, which had started like a cold trauma torture session, was now something I had become much more comfortable with. I had been rewarded with my best-ever distances covered in open water. At least in the shorter sessions, my desired speeds in the water and the bike were where they needed to be.

But it wasn't just about the physical training. This month had been a test of my mental strength. Sometimes during the long weeks, it can feel a little like the film *Groundhog Day*. Six months into this Ironman training saga, and with two more still on the horizon, my life started to resemble the plot of Bill Murray's almost endless time-loop film: no matter what the day of the week, I woke up to the same routine – swim, bike, run, eat, sleep, repeat. There was a certain comfort in the predictability. However, as much as I tried to spice things up, the same stretches of road on my runs, the familiar lanes of the swimming pool, the unchanging view from my turbo trainer, all started to become a little bit repetitive. I could see why Coach Garrie had reached out when he did. I can understand how, as the shine of Ironman training wears off, after six long months with the goal so close, but feeling so far, a lot of people find themselves at a crossroads. Continue to commit and charge through the monotony of it, or fall away?

Coach Garrie's step-up in the training plan was not just a challenge: it was an opportunity to prove to him and myself that I could handle whatever was thrown at me. It was a chance not just to prepare myself for the Ironman, both in terms of the physical challenge and the unexpected situations, but also to equip myself with discipline, commitment and sheer willpower that I would carry with me long after crossing the Ironman finish line. It was a reminder that to achieve something as monumental as an Ironman, you couldn't turn up on the day, nor could a mortal like me decide to do it three months out and get myself in a state to achieve this. You need to be willing to put in the work, to face your fears and to keep going, even when every fibre of your being is telling you to stop, or stay in that bed on those chilly spring mornings.

The journey ahead was still long, the road to Ironman still fraught with challenges. But I was more ready than I had ever been. I had fallen off the wagon, but got back on and delivered. I had survived the initial step-up in training and peak training was well and truly up and running. In doing these things, I had stepped up, as an athlete, as a person, and as a future Ironman.

Chapter 25
Bolton Bound –
The Ironman Training Weekend

In a year when my social calendar was as barren as a desert thanks to a cocktail of Covid restrictions on social gatherings and an Ironman training schedule tighter than a triathlon suit, receiving an invite from Coach Garrie felt like spotting an oasis. It wasn't just any invite, mind you. This was a golden ticket to an Ironman training weekend in Bolton, the very heartland of our upcoming race. There is not a lot that can perk up and excite a man after four months of non-stop training, but this was it.

Garrie's invite promised a weekend that was part learning, part real-time course experience. A chance to trade the solitary confinement of my training for a group setting, to learn not just from Garrie, but from fellow Ironman aspirants. This was in itself quite exciting. All my interactions with Garrie had been digital – whether calls, Zoom or messaging – beyond one cycle meet-up, ditto with the WhatsApp group of triathletes. It would be a gathering of newbies, all of us green in our Ironman journey, each harbouring dreams and doubts about the race in July. This included some of the fellow newbies from the group, and others who had found the training weekend online.

The weekend oozed experience. Coach Garrie, as discussed, is an Ironman veteran, but it was jointly hosted by his partner – herself a two-time Bolton finisher – plus another coach who had passed the finish line at the end of the red carpet of the Ironman UK just a few years prior.

The weekend's itinerary would combine physical training with classroom sessions which promised to be a goldmine of information, covering everything from race-day strategies to nutrition. But it was the opportunity to experience the course first-hand that set my heart racing. To swim in the waters of Pennington Flash again, a fresh chance to cycle the undulating Lancashire roads away from my monitor and to run the paths of the Bolton marathon route. It was like a dress rehearsal for the main event.

I immediately thought of inviting Max, my fellow Ironman-in-training. However, Max, juggling the heroic feats of parenthood, just couldn't commit to three days away from family life. Understandable, yet the introvert in me didn't like to tackle these things alone. However, with parenting duties not due until October, I had no such excuse.

The prospect of the training weekend was thrilling. Rather than rocking up on 4 July, facing the Ironman course with fresh eyes, we'd get a backstage pass to the Ironman's inner workings: an opportunity to peel back the curtain and see what really goes in to preparing for such an event. The idea of meeting a dozen or so fellow first-timers added to the allure. I imagined us as a band of warriors, each on our own quest, coming together for a weekend of shared learning and camaraderie.

As Friday evening rolled in, I found myself walking into a small Italian restaurant on the outskirts of Bolton, the chosen venue for our meet-up. The first thing that struck me, even before the aromas of garlic and basil, was the vibrant noise and buzz of what I had expected to be a quiet local restaurant. It was a stark contrast to the lockdown life I'd become accustomed to. The hostess had seated our group at a couple of outdoor tables, and while the laughter and hum of conversation filled the space around us, it felt both exhilarating and slightly disconcerting, a reminder of the world slowly waking up from its pandemic-induced slumber.

The second thing I noticed when we were seated, is how easy it had been to spot this very special group. Due to a lack of annual leave, I'd had to race straight from the office, where meetings were littered with people peacocking with

Rolex, Omega and Tudor watches. Here every single person had an oversized Garmin attached to their wrist. This was not your usual gathering!

The group assembled for the weekend was a diverse tapestry of individuals, united by a single goal but varied in every other way. As I looked around, I half-expected to find a gathering of chiselled athletes, each resembling a Greek god or goddess. I was pleasantly surprised to find a motley crew that spanned ages, genders and locations across the country, from Aberdeen to Devon. It was a reassuring reminder that the Ironman challenge was relatively inclusive.

The dinner was full of warmth, laughter and carbs. Let's face it, pizza and pasta will always be a hit with a bunch of people putting the hours in that we were. Conversations flowed as easily as the beer and wine, with each of us sharing our training escapades, mishaps and the roads (both literal and metaphorical) that had led us here. There were tales of early morning swims that felt more like polar plunges, long bike rides that turned into unexpected adventures and runs that tested both the spirit and the soles of our shoes.

It was fascinating to hear the diversity in our journeys. For some, Ironman was a bucket-list challenge, a tick-off on a list of life's adventures. For others, it was a journey of transformation, a path to reclaim health, or a quest for self-discovery. As we shared our deepest fears about the course – the notorious hills of the bike route, the unpredictability of open-water swimming or the daunting final marathon run – a sense of solidarity formed. Each confession, each shared anxiety, wove a thread of camaraderie among us.

At the end of the night, we said our goodbyes, already bonded, and ready to meet up the next day to face our first in-field experience: a Saturday morning dip in the location of the Ironman swim, Pennington Flash.

Arriving at Pennington Flash early that next morning, there was a palpable buzz of excitement mixed with nerves.

As we geared up in our wetsuits, we were told our first Ironman hack – the strategic use of a plastic bag to slide our feet through the tight neoprene. It was one of those small yet ingenious tips that seasoned triathletes pass down to us newbies, a trick that saved minutes and a fair bit of wrestling.

Pennington Flash, primarily a boating lake, didn't allow swimming along the actual Ironman route during normal weekends, but a designated section was marked out for swimmers, patrolled by staff in canoes to rescue anyone who found themselves in any difficulty. As I zipped up my wetsuit and adjusted my goggles, I couldn't help but remember that this very lake was where my bout with bacterial pneumonia had begun. I pushed the apprehension aside, determined not to let past experiences cloud this opportunity.

The water of Pennington Flash was a stark contrast to the more familiar, filtered waters of Salford Quays. As we trudged down the muddy, sludgy pontoon towards our designated entry point assigned to swimmers mad enough for an early morning dip, it was clear that we were in for a more 'authentic' open-water experience. The water here was murkier, with visibility significantly lower than I was used to. A few ducks paddled nonchalantly nearby, seemingly amused by the procession of wetsuit-clad humans invading their space.

Despite the less-than-ideal water quality and visibility, we plunged in for an hour of thrashing and learning. This swim was less about perfect strokes and more about acclimatising to the environment: the unpredictability of open water, the limited visibility and the natural elements that made this outdoor swim such a unique challenge.

Coach Garrie and the other instructors patrolled the water's edge, offering tips on technique and answering our barrage of questions. They reminded us of the importance of sighting, of staying relaxed in the water and of maintaining an efficient stroke despite the distractions and challenges of the open environment.

After an hour our time was up. It had felt both exhilarating and exhausting. We peeled ourselves out of the water, each of us a little more confident, a little more prepared for what awaited us on section one of race day. We dragged our shivering bodies up the muddy pontoon, making a beeline for the shelter of the small onsite cafe, where warm drinks, Mars bars and a debrief awaited us.

As we huddled around steaming cups of tea and coffee, we shared our experiences of the water. Some had come from a seasoned swimming background – other challenges awaited them later on in the Ironman race – and so had ripped through the water at speed. Others had almost literally frozen in the water, their training so far confined to heated swimming pools, so this had been a stark reminder of how different the challenge of open-water swimming was. Still, whether a good or bad experience of Pennington, it was better to get a realisation of where we all stood.

As we all peeled off our wetsuits and chucked our goggles and swim caps in the boots of our cars there was a sense of accomplishment and camaraderie. We had tackled the waters of Pennington Flash together, now we were off for a little bit of classroom learning.

Chapter 26
Ironman 101 – The Training Weekend, Part Two

Fresh from our open-water swim at Pennington Flash, our group of Ironman hopefuls reconvened in a makeshift classroom in Bolton leisure centre. It felt like a flashback to my university days, when cramming sessions were as vital as the exams themselves. Except, in this case, the exam was Ironman UK, scheduled for 4 July, and the cramming was about absorbing as much Ironman wisdom as possible.

The next few hours were an Ironman masterclass, led by Coach Garrie and his team. It was like opening a treasure chest of knowledge, each piece of advice a gem that could make all the difference on race day. We delved into the nitty-gritty details of the event itself, gleaning the kind of practical tips you would expect from locals and veterans from past events. We discussed things like where to park on the morning of the swim and the best spots for friends and family to cheer us on along the course.

Nutritional advice flowed as freely as water at an aid station, covering everything from what to eat in the lead-up to the race, to the best fuelling strategies on the bike and run. We discussed clothing choices, transitioning techniques and how best to tackle the infamous Lancashire hills. It was a barrage of information, but every bit was crucial – these were the insights that books and online forums couldn't provide.

But the biggest revelation for me came with the discussion of the special needs bags – a concept that was new to many of us. Coach Garrie explained that these bags were our lifeline, a chance to have personal items, be it nutrition, spare inner tubes or emergency sticking plasters, available to us at specific points on both the bike and run course if we requested them. It was like discovering a hidden feature in a video game – a strategic advantage that could potentially make a huge difference. These needed to be requested on registration, so without this insider information it would not have been something I would ever have considered. My mind went to what treats I'd welcome come the start of that final loop of the bike course, or on the final laps of the marathon.

As the day wrapped up, my mind, rather than my body, felt exhausted with the sheer volume of information: it was overwhelming, but in the best way possible. I packed up my notes and gear, my head buzzing with race strategies, nutrition plans and the new-found knowledge of special needs bags.

As the afternoon sun cast long shadows over Bolton, our group geared up for a practical run around the actual Ironman marathon course. We converged in Bolton town centre, parking near Queen's Park, which, in a few months, would transform into the bustling hub of Transition 2. Here, we would hopefully be changing from cycling to running, a pivotal moment in the Ironman race. Our guide for the day gave us a brief walking tour of the park, outlining the expanse that would soon be swarming with athletes, supporters and volunteers.

The idea of running four laps around Bolton as part of the Ironman course seemed daunting, but today was a manageable single lap of the course at a steady pace. The run through Bolton's cobbled streets was a journey through the town's heart. The iconic town hall was destined to be a landmark on race day. We'd be planning to do this part of the journey four times before running down the finishing chute positioned at the foot of the steps. However, the tranquillity was abruptly disrupted as we encountered an unexpected scene – a protest, with its participants loud and impassioned. The atmosphere swiftly shifted from casual training to an adrenaline-fuelled dash, our pace inadvertently matching that of race day as we navigated through the unexpected hostile crowd in front of us.

As we cut through Queen's Park, the reality of the course's topsy-turvy gradients became evident. The incline, which we would face four times over on race day, was a subtle reminder of the challenge that lay ahead. It was clear that the hilly nature of the park would be beyond a test of endurance; it would be a real test of the spirit.

Running down the bustling Chorley Road, flanked by pubs and passed by constant traffic, I confess it wasn't the most enticing of routes. However, with a little bit of imagination and squinting of the eyes, you could just about conjure the energy and excitement that would fill these streets come July. The thought of crowds cheering, music playing and the announcer's voice booming as we ran this very route filled me with a mix of excitement and nervous anticipation.

As we completed our lap and made our way back to Queen's Park, the day's run served as a valuable preview of what awaited us. It wasn't just about logging miles; it was about visualising the race, feeling the course under our feet and mentally preparing for the task ahead. The pace was slow enough that we could use the time to swap stories of our current running training and thoughts on the weekend so far.

Exhausted yet exhilarated, we gathered our thoughts and our gear. Today's run had been an eye-opener – a peek into the future, a taste of the Ironman experience. As I packed up, my mind replayed the route, embedding the turns, the landmarks and the inclines into my memory.

The dawn of a new day marked the final chapter of our Ironman training weekend. This was a day dedicated to another hands-on experience: the Ironman cycle loop, the first in-person attempt since my early year jaunt when I had left the course a little bruised and battered. We assembled in the car park of the Bolton Wanderers stadium, on a Sunday morning: it was an odd sight to see it temporarily taken over by a congregation of triathletes and their two-wheeled steeds. It was a moment to become a bit envious of others, as we compared the various bike set-ups. Some had opted for the aerodynamic allure of tri-bikes, while others, like myself, had chosen the familiar reliability of road bikes.

As we set off, I could feel a new-found confidence that had been absent during my previous attempt at this route. One of the biggest advantages of my Sunday sessions on Rouvy was the mental roadmap of the course I now had etched into my mind. Where once I had been guessing the end of gruelling hills and wasting mental energy hoping for the next flat or descent, I now had a strategic understanding of when to conserve energy and when to push hard. Houses and other landmarks en route now seemed familiar and marked the different stages of the course.

Our bunch of Ironman wannabes naturally divided into three subgroups. There were the speed demons, who seemed to slice through the course with effortless grace, clearly confident in their abilities and who would be a force on race day on the course. At the other end were the more cautious cyclists, for whom every pedal stroke was a calculated effort, as they were still not feeling the most confident with this particular discipline. I found myself in the third group, comfortably nestled between the two extremes. The ride was not just a physical test, it was a lesson in technical skills. Descending hills at 30mph was a whole different ball-game in reality compared to the digitised version I'd become so used to. Every turn and descent was a delicate dance of balance, speed and nerve.

Upon completing the loop and regrouping in the car park, the first group, undaunted and eager, decided to embark on a second lap. The invitation to join was tempting, but I was content with the knowledge and experience gained from the day's ride. I politely declined, choosing instead to pack up my bike and reflect on the weekend's learnings.

Driving away from the stadium, my mind replayed the events of the three days. From the open-water swim at Pennington Flash to the classroom sessions and the real-world experience of the run and cycle routes, every moment had been an invaluable piece of my Ironman puzzle. I had not only gained practical insights into the race but also connected with fellow athletes, each on their own journey to Ironman glory.

It felt like the road to Ironman UK was becoming clearer and this weekend had been a big accelerator of that. The training, the learning and the experiences had brought me a step closer to the starting line. The physical training for Ironman is daunting, but understanding the logistics and nuances of the race is equally critical. As I contemplated the weeks ahead, I felt a surge of anticipation and determination. This weekend had been challenging, enlightening and profoundly rewarding: a weekend crash-course in Ironman 101. As I closed this chapter, I did so with a heart full of gratitude and a mind focused on the finish line that awaited in July.

Chapter 27

In it for the Long Run – Rethinking the Pace

As the Ironman training continued, the extent to which Coach Garrie had influenced my approach to running had become quite evident. When he first took the reins of my training, he was faced with a glaring issue in my running regime – every run, irrespective of its nature, was executed at a high-octane intensity. From the Malta 10k to my daily lockdown trots along the canal, each outing was treated as a sprint rather than a marathon, metaphorically speaking. There had been no space for pace management or slow recovery runs. Despite clocking more than 100 miles each month during lockdown, my body had paid a steep price for this unbridled enthusiasm – exhaustion and constant little niggles and soreness lurking in the shadows.

Garrie's first order of business was to introduce me to the concepts of aerobic and anaerobic workouts, two terms that would revolutionise my running strategy. Aerobic workouts, he explained, were all about endurance. They involved running at a pace where oxygen supply was sufficient, emphasising stamina and energy efficiency. These were the long, steady runs where conversation was possible and the heart wasn't hammering against the ribcage. In contrast, anaerobic workouts were the high-intensity runs, where the oxygen demand outstripped the supply and the body relied on stored energy sources. These were the sprints, the hill repeats – shorter, but incredibly intense sessions.

The distinction was eye-opening. No longer could my training just be about pounding the pavement with all my might, measured purely in miles accumulated. Now it was about understanding the physiology behind the run. This new strategy required a more nuanced approach, one that balanced endurance with intensity, giving equal importance to building stamina as well as speed.

The next critical piece of Coach Garrie's running puzzle was the concept of heart-rate zones. These zones, calculated based on my maximum heart rate, were a guide to how hard I should be pushing myself on different runs. Zone 1 was the light, almost leisurely jog – the 'warm-up' zone. Zone 2 was the aerobic zone, where I should spend most of my training hours, building endurance without overtaxing the body. Zone 3 was the moderate intensity level, a notch higher in effort but still sustainable. Zone 4 was where things got serious – the threshold zone, pushing the limits of aerobic capacity. And finally, Zone 5 – the anaerobic zone, short bursts of all-out effort, the territory of gasping breaths and burning muscles. I had been used to dancing around the upper limits when it came to zones; now I had to become a master of the low intensity.

This heart-rate based training was a game-changer. It transformed my runs from mere distance-covering exercises to strategic, purpose-driven workouts, focusing on quality over quantity. I began to view each run not just as a specific task, but a session with a defined outcome to achieve. This differed run to run, depending on what Coach Garrie had cooked up for me.

Adapting to this new approach wasn't easy. Slowing down felt counterintuitive at first, and monitoring my heart rate added a layer of complexity to what had always been a 'just run' approach. But as the weeks passed, the benefits became undeniable. I was running more, yet feeling less fatigued. My endurance was improving and the niggling pains that had often accompanied my high-intensity-only approach were fading away. I started to pack in as many miles as I had done previously, layered on with the additional bike (and more recently) swim workouts, but with none of the body trauma and injuries of before.

The long run, once a daunting prospect, became a meditative experience. These runs were no longer about how fast I could go but how smartly I could manage my energy, how effectively I could pace myself. They became journeys of self-discovery, an ego check and an opportunity to listen to my body while revelling in the sheer joy of running.

By the time May rolled around, my midweek runs had settled into a pattern of predominantly anaerobic workouts, sprinkled with dashes of high-intensity hill repeats or sprints. These sessions were my midweek bursts of energy, a chance to push the boundaries and test my limits in short, sharp bursts, and pocket-sized in time, so perfect to slot around my work schedule. But the real magic of my training unfolded at the end of the working week.

Friday nights had transformed from the typical end-of-week wind-down to the pinnacle of my running week. These runs were about endurance, about maintaining a consistent effort with a low intensity – a feat that required a focus and discipline akin to a military operation. Time was an afterthought; the goal was to hit Coach Garrie's mileage targets, regardless of how long it took. My determination to adhere to the lower heart-rate zones was almost comical in its dedication. I recall one night, in a moment of desperation, veering off the track to find a bush for a bathroom break, causing a brief spike in my heart rate. Later as I scanned my Garmin data to see how I had performed I realised the impact of my needed detour. I sent an apologetic and slightly embarrassed explanation to Garrie, who was both amused and impressed by my dedication to maintaining the desired heart-rate zone, albeit probably not keen for me to make sharing my bathroom trips a regular occurrence.

This new training ritual meant retiring the early morning half-marathon-plus distances I used to tackle before work. I'm dedicated, but not 4am dedicated. Instead, Friday evenings became sacred, reserved for my long-distance

The medal. With its majestic lion.

2021

IRONMAN®
UK ⚡ BOLTON
ENGLAND
2.4m Swim • 112m Bike • 26.2m Run

Posing with the Ironman truck at registration. It was all sunshine two days before …

All smiles! Clearly feeling good at this point.   *Less smiles ... the emotional journey that was the Ironman.*

Entering the Ironman village for registration.

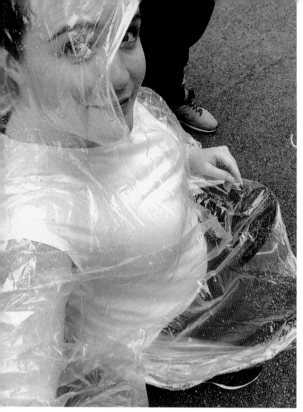

My biggest cheerleader. Briony shielding from the rain in Queens Park.

Here we go. Mask on, as we approach the water to commence the Ironman.

Someone's been to the merch tent! Max proudly showing his new Ironman cap.

The moment of calm before the storm. Briony, Craig and I.

IRONMAN England
21m · 🌐

Good news, we have successfully worked through the Safety Advisory Group process for IRONMAN UK, Bolton. We have received full stakeholder support to move forward with the event as planned. We will be implementing our 'Return to Racing' guidelines on the 4th July taking into account prevailing national and local public heath guidelines.

After a long year, we are more than excited to welcome you all back to the Supersapiens IRONMAN UK! Let's go!! 🏃

#IRONMAN
#ANYTHINGISPOSSIBLE

We are on! The Facebook post announcing that Ironman UK was happening.

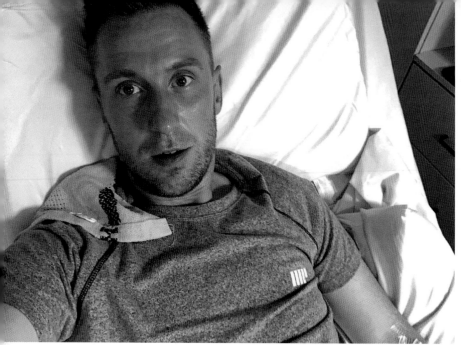

Where it all began. In a hospital bed, with an IVF. A sweaty, coughy, mess.

Another green week! Coach Garrie will be happy, as he reviews my training week.

The road to recovery. Literally weeks before lockdown, Briony and I celebrating our half marathons in Malta.

The last big swim complete … but I may need to loosen those goggles.

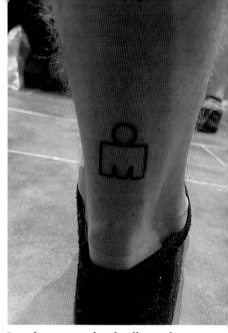

It took two years, but finally got the traditional Ironman tattoo.

The image sent to Max. The red carpet we hoped to cross in less than 48 hours' time.

runs. The routine became locked in. I'd finish work, park at home and then immediately transition into my running gear. I took an out-and-back, traffic-free route, starting from Timperley, to Altrincham via the canal, then joining the Trans Pennine Trail to Lymm, before returning home. It had all become as familiar as the back of my hand.

As the miles stretched and the sessions edged closer to marathon distances, my post-run recovery strategy evolved too. Uber Eats became an unexpected ally in my Ironman journey. I perfected the mid-run, one-handed order. If I timed it just right, I could meet the delivery just as I staggered through the door around 8:30pm, tired but triumphant. Just enough time to fuel up and hit bed ahead of the next morning's swim meet.

These Friday night runs were more than just training; they were adventures in their own right. Each run was a journey through quiet streets and serene trails, under the changing hues of the evening sky of late spring. As I pounded the pavement, week after week, these runs became meditative. The rhythmic sound of my footsteps, the steady beat of my heart and the focus on maintaining a low heart rate created a trance-like state. The necessity to train without music (headphones are prohibited in all Ironman races) forced me to be more present. In doing so, without the blaring of noughties dance songs, I found a sense of calm and peace, a sense of purpose and direction to my training.

As May drew its curtains to a close, my training log boasted an impressive feat – the long runs had reached a peak of at least 17 miles, all comfortably nestled within the reassuring boundaries of Zone 1 and 2. This was no minor victory, it was a testament to the evolution of my running thanks to Coach Garrie and the hours put in, a symbol of the endurance I had painstakingly built over the months.

Gone were the days of haphazard, high-intensity sprints that left me more depleted than energised. Now, each run was a deliberate, calculated effort – a dance with my heart rate, a harmonious blend of distance and discipline. These runs weren't just about covering miles; they were about mastering the art of sustainable effort, about finding a rhythm that could carry me through the marathon leg without burning out.

I had transformed from a runner who simply clocked up miles for the sake of it, to an athlete who understood the nuances of pace, effort and endurance. The 17-mile runs, once a daunting prospect, had become a space where I found my stride, both literally and metaphorically. The run portion of the Ironman, which had once loomed large as a formidable challenge, now felt like familiar territory, a path I had trodden and re-trodden, each step taking me closer to readiness. I had grown to learn to listen to my body, to respect the ebb and flow of energy that would be required on the day and to maintain a pace that would be challenging yet sustainable come 4 July.

The journey to this point had been long, filled with early mornings, late nights and endless miles, but it had brought me to a place of readiness for the final month ahead. I was feeling more prepared for the marathon leg of the Ironman, ready to put to the test all that I had learned and trained for … as long as I could get past the swim and bike first.

Chapter 28
Pedalling Through Fears – My Evolution on the Bike

As my Ironman journey reached its last few months, one element loomed over me like a colossal shadow – the cycling portion. Despite making strides in swimming and gaining confidence in my running, the bike leg of the Ironman was my personal Goliath. It wasn't just about the physical challenge; it was the mental hurdle of spending the majority of race day pedalling. In the world of Ironman, particularly in the hilly terrain around Bolton, the bike section was notorious for its high rate of DNFs (Did Not Finish). If anything was going to trip me up, it was most likely going to be this.

The countless hours I had initially invested during lockdown, sweating away on my turbo trainer in the solitary confinement of my home, seemed like a lifetime ago. Back then, Zwift races and Coach Garrie's structured training sessions were my sole companions as I pedalled in place, going nowhere yet training for something monumental. These sessions were my introduction to cycling endurance, a foundation upon which my Ironman bike journey was built. The roads of Bolton had seemed a lifetime away.

However, as lockdown eased and the world slowly opened up, the months to Ironman had flown by. The turbo trainer sessions gave way to the real deal – long rides through the picturesque Cheshire countryside. These rides became the cornerstone of my Sunday mornings. It became a ritual that saw me chasing the sunrise at my required pace, winding through quiet country lanes before the traffic had a chance to get going.

These outdoor rides were a different beast compared to the virtual miles on Zwift. The unpredictable weather, the varying terrains and the occasional navigational mishap added layers of complexity and adventure to my training. The ease of watching the latest Netflix series on my phone while pedalling at home was replaced by the constant need to be paying attention to the conditions and the unforgiving cars on my journey.

But with every mile conquered, every hill summited, and every long ride completed, my confidence grew. I started to understand the rhythm of long-distance cycling – the importance of pacing, the art of fuelling on the go and the mental game of keeping the pedals turning when every muscle fibre screamed for respite.

Yet despite any improvements I was seeing, it was the bike portion of the Ironman that at times literally kept me up at night. Unlike the swim and the run, where it was me and just a wetsuit and some running trainers (with hopefully a bit more clothing!), I was aware the cycle portion was just as much about machine as man. The nature of the bike itself meant, as good as I could be on the day, one mechanical mishap would mean my race was run. There were things I had to address to reduce the risk.

One of the initial hurdles I faced was getting to grips with clip-on shoes. Commonly used in cycling for their efficiency in transferring power from the leg to the pedal, these shoes literally clip the rider's feet to the bike, ensuring every ounce of effort is converted into forward motion. However, the art of clipping in and out of the pedals was something that initially seemed as complex as quantum physics to me.

In my previous life in London, I had been determined to master this skill, only to find myself intimately acquainted with the concrete of Wandsworth and Putney on one too many occasions. Failing to unclip in time turned simple stops into embarrassing, and sometimes painful, mishaps. At that time, the cycling shoes were sent packing to the local charity shop, and my bruised body and ego promised to never repeat this failed experiment. Those memories were etched in my mind, but there was no getting away from it: with eight hours to complete a 112-mile navigation of Bolton, I needed every advantage I could get.

Another element that sent shivers down my spine was the very real fear of punctures. Bolton's roads, notorious for their potholes, seemed to lie in wait for unsuspecting cyclists like me. The likelihood of suffering a puncture during the race was not just a possibility, it was a probability. The embarrassment of a DNF due to my inability to swiftly change an inner tube was a scenario I desperately wanted to avoid.

Determined to minimise this risk, I invested in what were claimed to be bomb-proof Continental race tyres. These were complemented by inner tubes that boasted self-healing gloop – the promise was, these were the cycling equivalent of a magic potion. I wasn't taking any chances.

This led to my weekly ritual, performed post bike-cleaning. I would practise replacing my inner tubes and use CO_2 canisters for quick tyre inflation. On more than one occasion, my inexperience with the canisters resulted in a loud bang, an exploded inner tube and a startled me. These mishaps, while frustrating, were invaluable lessons in the nuances of bike maintenance and repair. It was better to get it all out now, rather than have a mishap on mile 100 on the day.

These elements – mastering clip-on shoes and preparing for potential punctures – were as much a part of my Ironman training as the miles I logged on the bike. They were reminders that in a race as complex and demanding as an Ironman, it's not just about physical endurance and mental toughness; it's also about being prepared for all the possible outcomes and challenges of the day. I was trying to reduce the risk and slowly attempting to stack the odds in my favour.

As my Ironman journey progressed, I gradually succumbed to the persuasive powers of the gear gurus of the WhatsApp group and invested in a few additions to my bike to help me along the way. My trusty Boardman bike, which had started its life with me in a relatively humble state, began to undergo a series of transformations. While the dream of brand-new carbon wheels remained just that – a dream – (they were a non-starter as soon as I Googled how much they cost), instead I went for a slightly more budget-friendly pair of alloy wheels. This upgrade, though not as flashy as carbon, made a noticeable difference in the overall bike weight I had to heave up those hills.

Another significant addition to my cycling arsenal was the Garmin Edge 820 bike computer. It was like having a personal cycling analyst on board, providing me with data that helped fine-tune my training and strategies.

Following Coach Garrie's sage advice, I also revamped my hydration set-up. Gone was the front-heavy, cumbersome water carrier that had been a pain in the neck. In its place, I opted for two carbon bottle holders, accompanied by standard water bottles. This change not only reduced the weight on the front of the bike but also made for a much more comfortable and aerodynamic ride.

Amidst the rigours of my Ironman training, a regular new midweek adventure emerged, one that quickly became a highlight of my week. A few times a week during my lunch break, I would race to the bathroom, don the Lycra and sneak away for a rendezvous with the famed 'Wizard Climb' in Alderley. This wasn't just any hill: it was a mile-long ascent with a maximum gradient of 10.5 per cent, a perfect microcosm of the challenges waiting in Bolton.

The Wizard Climb became my personal training ground, a place to test my mettle against gravity. Each pedal stroke up that hill was a battle, a mix of determination and burning muscles. I would push myself, visualising the hills of Bolton, each climb a rehearsal for race day. The ascent was tough, no doubt, but it was the descent that truly added the thrill to this midweek escape.

Descending the Wizard Climb was about learning to embrace speed, to trust my bike and my instincts as I hurtled down at what felt like breakneck speeds. Each descent grew my confidence, teaching me the fine art of balancing caution with courage.

Then, at the bottom, I would pause, catch my breath and prepare to do it all over again. This repetition, this cycle of climb and descent, became a physical and mental exercise. It was not just about building leg strength or improving cardiovascular fitness, it was about sharpening my focus, about learning to find comfort in discomfort.

By the end of May, all these incremental changes and upgrades culminated in a significant milestone – a 92-mile ride that I completed in exactly six hours. This achievement was not just a matter of pride, it was a tangible measure of my progress. This sort of distance, which would have seemed insurmountable just a few short months ago, was now within my grasp.

Each pedal stroke on that 92-mile ride was a reflection of the journey I had been on – not just in terms of physical training but also in understanding and mastering the nuances of cycling for Ironman. Following my initial struggles around the bike course back at the start of the year, the bike leg had threatened to overtake the open water swim as my most feared discipline. But now it had evolved into something I approached with confidence and even a sense of anticipation.

The evolution of my journey on the bike was a microcosm of my overall Ironman journey – a progression from apprehension and uncertainty to confidence and readiness. It had required mastering new skills, using my support circle to push and advise me, and had needed the dedication of hours of practice to get me to where I was at. With each upgrade on my bike and every mile added to my training, I was inching closer to the start line, ready to pedal my way to (hopefully) Ironman success.

Chapter 29
The Uncertainty of Ironman Dreams

In the ever-turbulent world of Ironman training, amidst a global pandemic and preparing for becoming a dad, uncertainty had become a constant companion. By May, Max and I, united by our Ironman aspirations, had planned a 'boys' trip', although it was more Ironman than Ayia Napa – a weekend away in Nottingham for the Outlaw Half-Triathlon event.

The Outlaw Half, for the uninitiated, is a prestigious event in the UK triathlon calendar, offering a taste of the Ironman experience with half the distance. A relatively relaxed and favourable course compared to Bolton but an opportunity to test ourselves over a 1.2-mile swim, a 56-mile bike ride and a 13.1-mile run. It's at this stage in the Ironman training that athletes commonly dip their toes into the half-distance event, acclimatising to race conditions and gearing up for the more significant challenge that awaited us.

Max and I had everything lined up – hotel rooms were booked, our training schedules meticulously aligned and, thanks to Max's dad (a legend in his own right), a pickup truck at our disposal to transport our bikes and gear. The anticipation was palpable, the buzz of a real race, and a real yardstick in our training calendar. Plus, there was an added excitement after over a year of restrictions: a road trip, a new experience; this really felt like a turning point, returning to the old norm.

However, in a twist that was becoming all too familiar in these times, our plans were abruptly derailed. An email arrived, as unwelcome as a flat tyre on a smooth ride, announcing the cancellation of the Outlaw Half this year. The words on the screen blurred into a mess of disappointment – all our plans, our excitement, dashed in an instant. The cancellation, while understandable in the face of the ongoing pandemic, was a gut punch for the training and the mental lift I had hoped a good race-time would give me. Plus, the prospect of experiencing race conditions, of being in the mix with fellow triathletes, and the adrenaline rush of competition – all were now off the table.

As I processed the news, my thoughts immediately went to the bigger picture. Ironman UK – could that be next on the chopping block? The shadow of uncertainty loomed larger than ever. If smaller events were being cancelled, what did that mean for our main event? The thought of it being cancelled was too bitter a pill to swallow. The pandemic had taught us to expect the unexpected, to roll with the punches, but this felt different. It was a sobering reminder of how even the best-laid plans could be tripped up by forces way beyond our control.

Over the next few days, hotels were cancelled, bags were unpacked and emergency extra training sessions were dropped into the calendar to compensate for the loss of the race. Yet, the spectre of cancellations haunted me – not just our Outlaw Half plans, but the wider Ironman race calendar. The creeping dread of uncertainty was palpable, as rumours of the next race for the chop were thrown around the WhatsApp group.

In a move that sent ripples of worry through the triathlon world, our worst fears started to unfold. Ironman sent emails announced the postponement of six of its major races:

– Ironman 70.3 Marbella, originally scheduled for 25 April 2021, pushed to 19 September 2021

– Ironman 70.3 Venice-Jesolo, set for 2 May 2021, rescheduled to 26 September 2021

– Zafiro Ironman 70.3 Alcùdia-Mallorca, planned for 8 May 2021, with a new date still to be confirmed

- Ironman Mallorca, initially on 15 May 2021, now awaiting a new date

- Ironman 70.3 Aix en Provence, supposed to be on 16 May 2021, moved to 19 September, 2021.

- Ironman Lanzarote, slated for 22 May 2021, postponed to 3 July 2021.

Each postponement was a small echo of our own disappointment. You felt for those triathletes who had trained long and hard, who would now have to reset their training and start again some months later. But it was the delay of Ironman Lanzarote, slated just six weeks before our Ironman UK, that struck a particularly resonant chord. The uncertainty was no longer a distant concern; it was knocking on the door of our own race. I had to recognise that, for me, the practicality of a race later on would not be feasible. Briony had been an amazing supporter of my journey so far, putting up with my training schedules, my bags of dirty training gear and having a zombie for a husband for months now. That was all with the promise that this had a very clear end-date in July; that, post-race, I'd return to my usual self, pivot my attention to where it was needed. There was now a genuine risk that this event could be moved to later on in the year. However, I knew that any movement from the original July date would be clashing with our other big journey, that trip to parenthood.

The wave of cancellations and postponements wasn't just confined to the international Ironman events, it was a storm that was sweeping across the entire endurance sports landscape and reaching the UK. The uncertainty and disappointment we felt was echoed closer to home as major races in our own backyard faced similar fates. The Manchester and London marathons, iconic events in the UK's running calendar, were not immune to the disruptions caused by the pandemic. Both races were pushed to later in the year, adding to the growing list of disrupted events as my anxiety grew. Manchester, my home, was just 40 miles away from Bolton – it was all just getting a little too close for comfort.

Each deferred race added to the collective anxiety within the triathlon community, and questions began to swirl. Would Ironman UK meet the same fate? Were our months of training about to be rendered moot?

Amidst all the swirling rumours and uncertainties, there emerged a whisper of a potential solution amongst the Facebook groups, the WhatsApp groups and the forums. One that harked back to a previous Ironman event in 2018. Back then, local fires forced the organisers to make a significant but necessary last-minute alteration: they shortened the bike course from the standard 112 miles to 95 miles. This 17-mile reduction, though seemingly small in the grand scheme of an Ironman, was a major deviation from the traditional format. Now, as I grappled with the possibility of cancellations and postponements, a precedent lingered in the air. Would we get a shortened course, would they reduce the numbers or would a whole discipline disappear? Would any of this be a better or worse solution to a delay in the race or in fact a race cancellation? It was a question that gnawed at me, a debate between the practicalities of the situation: the battle between just wanting to get it done now, versus the ideals I had set for myself. The full Ironman distance was a badge of honour, a testament to one's endurance and willpower. To alter that, even by a mere 17 miles, felt like an asterisk on an otherwise unblemished record. I genuinely didn't know, rightly or wrongly, if I could call myself an Ironman if I didn't complete that full distance.

This period of uncertainty tested us in ways that no amount of physical training could. It was a mental and emotional marathon, a test of patience and resilience. The dream of crossing the Ironman finish line, which had once seemed so clear and tangible, now felt shrouded in mist.

But amidst this uncertainty, there was a silver lining – a lesson in adaptability and the power of hope. I had to learn to focus on the elements that were within my control – my training, my mindset, my preparation. Everything else, I realised, I couldn't control, so as best I could, I had to forget about it. Yes, the possibility of cancellation loomed large, but it also brought into sharp focus the reasons why I had embarked on this journey in the first place.

It wasn't just about the race day; it was about the journey – the early mornings, the late nights, the miles logged and the challenges overcome. Whether or not Ironman UK happened as planned, the journey itself had been transformative. I had grown stronger, physically, mentally and emotionally. The path to Ironman had become a metaphor for life – unpredictable, challenging, but ultimately rewarding.

As we navigated through this uncertain landscape that was race cancellations, vaccines and face masks, my training sessions became more than just physical exercises; they were acts of defiance against the unpredictability of the times. They were affirmations of my needed resilience and adaptability. Every run, every ride, every swim was a statement – that even in the face of uncertainty, I would continue to strive, to dream and to persevere. This was not the time to be concerned with situations outside of my control. I had to be ready on 4 July. The question that remained, would Ironman be ready for me?

Chapter 30
The Final Stretch – May Wrap-Up

As May drew to a close, the countdown to Ironman UK entered its final, crucial phase. We were on the cusp of June, the last month of training, a period that marked the culmination of Coach Garrie's gruelling peak training plan. One Sunday, as a mini celebration after I returned from my bike ride, Briony decided to indulge us in a rare treat – a celebratory Sunday meal out. I washed my bike down in record time and raced upstairs to get ready for a much-needed date with my wife. We chose San Carlo, a haven of Italian carb-fuelled culinary delights just a few miles down the road, perfect for a much-needed feast. As we settled into our outdoor seats, the atmosphere of the restaurant provided a soothing contrast to the rigorous discipline of training.

Briony, eating for two, selected her courses with a smile, while I, after months of intense training, felt like I was eating for at least five, and wolfed it down like a man who had just ended a hunger strike. We savoured each course, from the starter to the dessert, allowing ourselves to relax afterwards with a coffee, to enjoy the moment. It was a celebration of not just the amazing food but of the journey so far and a chance for me to reflect on the month just been.

Despite the ramp-up in training intensity, May surprisingly witnessed a resurgence in my commitment that had been wobbling. Of the seven-to-nine sessions scheduled each week, I only missed three throughout the entire month. This consistency was more than just a tick in the box, it was a testament to the dedication I had to get this journey done, to give it my all and get to that start line in my best possible shape. Each swim, bike and run was a step closer to that Ironman finishing line – a journey of sweat, grit and relentless determination.

Amidst a month full of the flurry of training sessions, one highlight stood out – the Ironman training weekend hosted by Coach Garrie and his friends. This experience had been a watershed moment in my preparation, a turning point that shifted my perspective from trepidation to anticipation. The weekend had not only bolstered my physical readiness but had given a significant boost to my mental game. It allowed me to visualise the race, to understand the rhythm and flow of what awaited me in Bolton.

The practical sessions, especially the bike ride around the actual course, had been invaluable. They had transformed abstract concepts, strategies and gradient maps into tangible experiences. Some of the hills that I had only seen on paper or a screen were now familiar challenges that I had conquered. The roads of Bolton, the home to one of my biggest tests early on in my training, were now etched in my memory, each turn and incline a known quantity, giving me the confidence to know I had climbed them all with energy in the bank. Pennington Flash, which had long held bad memories as the starting point to my bacterial pneumonia-plagued stay in Trafford hospital, was now associated with a positive time, swimming in there with good form.

But beyond the physical aspects, the weekend had been a mental boost: a convergence of minds and spirits, a gathering of individuals all united by a common goal. The camaraderie of the weekend, the shared experiences and the collective energy had been infectious. It wasn't just about the individual anymore, it was about being part of something larger – a community of athletes all striving towards the same daunting goal.

The tips shared over those two days – from nutrition hacks and transition tricks to secret bags only available on request – were more than just information. They felt like a secret weapon in my arsenal for race day. Knowledge, they say, is power, and those sessions had empowered me in ways

I hadn't anticipated. They had demystified the Ironman challenge, breaking it down into manageable segments, each with its own strategy and approach. It felt like it had started to slightly tip the odds in my favour.

As the final weeks of training for Ironman UK unfolded, I found myself reflecting on the transformative journey of each discipline. The progress was not just in numbers and times; it was a fundamental shift in how I approached and experienced each aspect of the triathlon.

Swimming, the discipline that I had such restricted access too, once my Achilles heel and my biggest fear, had morphed into a Saturday morning meditative retreat. The early days of struggle, and apprehension of those cold open waters, had given way to a serene synchronicity with the water. Outdoor swims had become a sanctuary, a time when I was truly disconnected from the world's distractions – no phones allowed here ... each stroke was a moment of mindfulness, a rhythmic meditation. This transformation was more than physical; it was a mental and emotional alignment with the water.

On the cycling front, the numbers spoke for themselves. Clocking up 92 miles in the saddle, I knew I was only 20 miles short of what would be required on race day. But it was more than just miles logged; it was about the quality of training. The countless ascents and descents of the Wizard Hill had been instrumental. They provided more than just physical conditioning, they imbued me with confidence for the climbs ahead and honed my technical skills for the descents. I had committed time to try and deconstruct any risks to my race day, from an energy drop to a flat tyre. Cycling was no longer just a segment of the Ironman, it was a journey of endurance, skill and resilience.

Running, the final act of the Ironman triathlon, had seen a significant evolution for me. From the early days of junk miles, high heart rates and a race against the clock, Coach

Garrie had rebuilt me as a master of low heart-rate running and it was a game-changer. Long runs, once a battle against fatigue and boredom, had become a disciplined exercise in patience and pace. I had learned to harness the power of running within this aerobic zone, finding a sweet spot where distance was covered efficiently without overtaxing my body. This skill was more than physical, it was a mental adaptation to the demands of endurance running. I was hoping that this mastery would translate seamlessly on race day. The question was whether I could replicate this efficiency after 114.4 miles of swimming and cycling.

As May waned and the calendar flipped, signalling the imminent approach of Ironman UK, I found myself at a crucial juncture of my training journey. The month had been gruelling. It had pushed me to the edge of my physical and mental limits, but it had also brought into sharp focus the final stretch of my preparation. Just two more weeks … two weeks of intensive training were etched into my diary, a final push to solidify the foundation I had built over the past seven long months. Beyond that lay the promise of a three-week taper, a period of reduced intensity designed to let my body recover and peak at just the right moment – race day.

However, the physical demands of May were only part of the story. The month had also been a roller-coaster ride of emotions, primarily due to the cancellation of our planned trip to Nottingham for the Outlaw Half. This event should have been a crucial milestone, a rehearsal for the main event, and its cancellation left a void in my preparation. More than the lost opportunity to test my readiness, it was a stark reminder of the uncertainty that still clouded Ironman UK. The biggest question of all still remaining unanswered: would Ironman UK be given the go-ahead?

With just 34 days to go until the big day, this uncertainty was the most significant challenge I faced, because it was simply out of my control. Training had become a routine, almost a comfort in its predictability, but the unpredictability over whether the race would go ahead was a constant mental strain. Every news alert, every email notification, carried the potential to either buoy my spirits or dash my hopes. All would have to reveal itself soon.

Despite these uncertainties, I clung to the hope that all the sweat, the early mornings, the late evenings and the sacrifices would culminate in the opportunity to stand at the starting line in Bolton. Each training session became an act of faith – in the process, in my coach's guidance and in the belief that the race would go ahead. I held on to the hope and the excitement for race day, ready to embrace whatever outcome awaited. The road to Ironman UK had been long and challenging, but it had led me to this point – prepared, hopeful and eager to face the final test.

Part Three: Ironman Preparation

Chapter 31

The Great Bike Service Saga

As Ironman UK edged closer, my trusty Boardman bike, which had been a stalwart companion through countless hours on the turbo trainer and the undulating Cheshire hills, was due for a well-earned service. Coach Garrie, ever the fount of sage advice, along with his cycle-savvy friends from the WhatsApp group, had recommended scheduling the service between four and six weeks out from the race itself. The timing was strategic – close enough to the Ironman to benefit from any tweaks and adjustments, yet far enough to address any post-service gremlins that might decide to make an appearance.

Confidently, I picked up the phone to book a service appointment, assured that it would be straightforward. After all, I had always managed to get my bike serviced without a hitch down the years, never waiting more than a few days. My first call was to the shop where I had previously had a bike fit – a place that knew my Boardman almost as well as I did. However, their response left me dumbfounded – no available slots for the next few months. Undeterred, I tried several other local bike shops, only to be met with the same frustrating answer.

It was then that I discovered a surprising side-effect of the pandemic – a government-introduced bike repair scheme coupled with a boom in bike sales, and the sheer volume of people digging out their old ones, had turned bike servicing appointments into a scarcity akin to a needle in a haystack. Every cyclist in the area, it seemed, had the same idea, and the shops were inundated with service requests, beyond what they could fulfil.

This revelation sent me into a mild panic. The thought of heading into Ironman UK with an unserviced bike was akin to walking a tightrope without a safety net – technically possible, but not advisable. My Boardman, while still in good shape, deserved a professional once-over, a bit of pampering to ensure it was in peak condition for the most challenging ride of its life (and mine).

In desperation, I expanded my search, calling shops further afield, hoping to find a hidden gem that hadn't been swamped by the sudden surge in cycling popularity. Each call was a mix of hope and anxiety, a roller coaster of emotions that only a triathlete in need of a bike service could understand. As the rejections piled up, my admiration for the humble bike mechanic grew exponentially. These unsung heroes of the cycling world were clearly in high demand, their skills and expertise more valuable than ever in these times of cycling fever. While it was great to see, I just needed one to have a spot and give the TLC my Boardman deserved.

Striking gold in the realm of bike servicing appointments felt akin to winning the lottery. At last, I secured a slot at one of the high street chains, a few towns away, but perfectly doable given the circumstances. With a sense of relief and triumph, I dropped my Boardman in the back of my car and drove there, eagerly anticipating the bike's return to glory. The very next day, it was back in my hands, gleaming as if it had just rolled off the showroom floor. I couldn't have been happier; it looked perfect and the feedback was positive. Some basic repairs had been done but nothing that would require parts to be shipped in. The gears shifted with a satisfying fluidity that brought a smile to my face. All seemed well in the world of cycling, or so I thought.

Disaster struck on its maiden voyage post-service, during the weekend's long ride. As I ramped up the speed and shifted into the higher gears, an unexpected problem reared its head. As the chain moved on to the top cog, it slipped off. The pedals spun freely, propelling nothing but my rising panic. I dismounted, I fixed the chain back on to the cog, and resumed riding, dismissing it as a one-off incident; these things happen right? However, the cycling gods seemed to have other plans. The chain slipped off again, turning my ride into a frustrating game of stop-and-start.

After the third incident within half an hour, I reluctantly abandoned my ride. However, instead of heading home, I found myself on a return journey to the bike shop, my mind clouded with concern. The repair man, a pleasant chap who had greeted me with a smile earlier, took my bike back into the workshop. A few minutes of tinkering, and he assured me that all was fixed. I returned home and decided to check myself that all was well once again. Yet, as I ventured out to resume my ride, the same issue cropped up. The chain stubbornly refused to cooperate, slipping off at every attempt to shift gears.

In usual circumstances, I would have headed straight back to the bike shop but with the day slipping away and having made a promise to Briony to go shopping for things the baby would need, I had no choice but to cut my ride short. For the whole drive to John Lewis (other retailers are available!) my mind wasn't on baby clothes or nursery themes; it was consumed with thoughts of my bike. The mechanical issues loomed large in my mind, casting a shadow over the upcoming Ironman. My once-trusted steed, maybe a little tired, but a reliable companion up until a few days ago, now felt like a liability. The fear of a DNF due to mechanical failure was a scenario I had never envisioned but it now seemed terrifyingly possible.

Despite the joyful nature of our plans, the rest of the day passed in a blur. As I accompanied Briony through the aisles of baby items, my thoughts were elsewhere, cycling through the possibilities of what could be wrong with the bike and how it could impact my race. The excitement of preparing for our new arrival was overshadowed by the nagging worry about my other baby – my bike. It was a stark reminder of how intertwined my Ironman journey had become with every aspect of my life. The mechanical issues with the Boardman were more than just a hiccup in training: they were a test of my ability to handle unexpected setbacks, to adapt and overcome. As I lay in bed that night, the problem of the slipping chain spun around in my mind, a puzzle that needed solving before I could face the starting line with confidence. The road to Ironman, it seemed, was never smooth, but it was these bumps along the way that tested and ultimately strengthened my resolve.

The saga of my Boardman bike and the shop that had serviced it morphed into a trilogy as I found myself making a third visit. The sleepless night had transformed my usual cheerful demeanour into a cocktail of sharpness tinged with desperation. The Ironman was fast approaching and my patience was wearing thin. I addressed the friendly mechanic with a more pleading tone, explaining the urgency of my predicament and the importance of the looming race.

With a nod of understanding, he took my bike back into the workshop. I waited, a bundle of nerves, hoping for a resolution. Yet, like a cruel replay, the same cycle reoccurred. The bike was passed back to me, reassurances were given, yet there I was again, on the side of the road, with a greasy chain in my hands and a growing sense of despair.

I berated myself for my lack of mechanical know-how, cursed my luck, and even questioned the competence of the seemingly unskilled mechanic. Desperation gnawed at me, leading to a last-minute call to my office for an afternoon off while I could think of a practical solution out of this mess. I hadn't come this bloody far to be derailed by a dodgy chain and an unskilled mechanic. I went for a new approach, and the bike was back in the boot of the car as I frantically drove to a local mechanic who had previously serviced my bike without issues. When I had initially enquired, he had no service appointments available, but seeing my ashen face and hearing the panic in my voice, he took pity on me.

Within moments of arriving at his shop, my local mechanic, my new-found hero, identified the problem. He mentioned something about derailleurs, but his words were a blur in the relief that washed over me. Someone had finally pinpointed the source of my frustration. In less than ten minutes, my Boardman was back in my hands, fixed and ready to go, with no charge for his time and expertise.

The moment I got home, I was back on the bike, taking no chances despite the reassuring words. The difference was palpable. Gear changing was smooth and effortless, the chain stayed firmly in place, and my hands remained grease-free – a significant victory. The joy of cycling returned in full force, the wind in my face, the road unfolding before me and my trusty bike responding beautifully to every command.

This entire episode felt like a lesson in problem solving, in seeking help when needed and in the kindness of strangers. The local mechanic, who stepped in when I was at my wit's end, was more than just a bike expert; he was a reminder that sometimes, the help we need comes from the most unexpected places.*

The bike issues had been a significant hurdle, but now, with my Boardman running smoothly, I felt a renewed sense of optimism. The countdown to Ironman UK continued, and I was back on track, ready to face whatever the race had in store. The journey had been tumultuous, but it had prepared me for the unpredictability of race day. I was ready, come what may, to take on the Ironman challenge.

*Side note – approximately 18 months later, I ran into the bike mechanic in a shop in town. It was literally like running into a hero, and in fact I had. I told him how much he had saved me that day (financially, mentally and, spoiler alert … my race). I only add this as in the heat of the moment of the bike repair, I didn't have the chance to truly convey this, and it is too common in life you miss these opportunities. If you are reading this, bike mechanic based out of a certain well-known chain in Manchester, you sir, are an absolute legend.

Chapter 32

The Final Push – Two Weeks of Peak Training

There we were, the start of June, and I was entering the final two weeks of peak training for Ironman UK. I thought it would be enlightening, perhaps even amusing, to give you a blow-by-blow account of what it's like to train under the watchful eye of Coach Garrie. Buckle up; it's quite a ride!

Week 1

Monday:

The week kicked off with what I affectionately called 'Monday Morning Madness' – a 40-minute pool session at an ungodly hour. I ideally liked to get these swimming sessions done early, to avoid any chance of a work or home emergency giving me the excuse to duck the session. The focus was on technique over speed or distance so I am not sure what distance I really covered, but it was all about concentrating on the total immersion swimming technique.

Tuesday:

Lunchtime rolled around, and it was time to hit the pavement. The run's breakdown was precise: a five-minute warm-up, 30 minutes in the dreamy Zone 2, then a 20-minute burst at a more race-like pace, capped with a five-minute cooldown. I covered seven miles, a satisfying distance; slower than I would have achieved in my old life, but this was all about control, and the miles felt comfortable.

Wednesday:

Ah, the enforced rest day! Thanks to the bike saga detailed in the previous chapter, I got an unexpected break. Although the twist was, this meant a double session was looming ominously on the horizon.

Thursday:

The bike was back, and it was time for hill reps – a phrase that had been sending shivers down my spine. I revisited the Wizard Hill in Alderley during lunch and followed Coach Garrie's instructions to challenge myself with four-minute climbs up the steep hill, followed by a swift descent and repeat. Six times I tackled this beast, covering just under ten miles in total. It wasn't about distance today; it was about conquering those hills.

Friday Morning:

The morning saw me back on the turbo trainer – a much simpler undertaking, as it involved a trip to the spare room, rather than lugging my bike and equipment in the car. I had learned to love the small, simple victories in my training calendar!

It began with a five-minute warm-up, I then went through the levels: 25 minutes in Zone 1, another 25 minutes in Zone 2, and yet another 25 minutes in Zone 3, followed by a five-minute cooldown. I notched up 27 miles in just under 1.5 hours, a far cry from Thursday's hill extravaganza. This was more like the speed which would be required in a little over four weeks' time.

Friday Evening:

Back from work by 6pm, running shoes on by 6:15, a quick kiss for Briony and bump knowing they would be asleep when I returned from my long run. This time, it was 17 miles in Zone 2, completed in 2 hours and 47 minutes. My reward? Meeting my Uber Eats driver at the door at 9pm for a well-deserved dinner before I headed to bed ahead of the next morning's session.

Saturday:

With Briony now noticeably pregnant, she was sitting out her once-regular runs, which meant I headed to Salford Quays at Media City for my 8:30am swim slot alone. I was in my element in the water by this stage, really starting to enjoy these sessions, clocking 1.8 miles in 1 hour and 10 minutes. The pace boded well for race day, potentially getting me out of the water in about 1 hour 20 to 1 hour 30 minutes.

Sunday:

The bike, now fully recovered from its mechanical ailments, was ready for some serious mileage. Coach Garrie's mandate was clear: time in the saddle. A whopping six hours required! I covered 92 miles and nearly 8,000 feet of climbing, a feat made slightly more bearable in the virtual world of Rouvy as I completed the three loops of the Ironman course, a big psychological lift. The pace averaged around 15mph, a comforting thought as it should keep me well clear of the dreaded cut-off. I knew it was going to be much more difficult on race day. Real world conditions meant that I would be unlikely to be descending the hills with the confidence I had today, and there was no risk of a puncture in my virtual laps. However, the nutrition and hydration seemed to be on point.

Week 2

Monday:

After Sunday's marathon bike session, I embraced this rest day with open arms. My legs thanked me, and I spent the day basking in the glory of doing absolutely nothing athletic. This was one of the true benefits of having Coach Garrie in my corner, reminding me to take the break when needed. Mind you, I had a right waddle as I moved around the office.

If I was this bad after a little over 90 miles, I dreaded to think what I would be like when the race itself was all over.

Tuesday:

Life, as it often does, threw a wrench into my well-oiled training plan. A lunchtime 40-minute swim session at the pool was abruptly truncated to a mere 20 minutes, thanks to a work emergency. Remember what I said last week? Always get these sessions in early Chris! Just as I was getting into the groove, the real world reminded me of its existence, and I had to scramble back to the office for an essential meeting. So much for escaping into the tranquil world of laps and strokes!

Wednesday:

Back on track with another hour-long run session. It started with the now-familiar five-minute warm-up, followed by 20 blissful minutes in Zone 2. But then came the kicker – 25 minutes at a faster, more aggressive race pace. This extended push resulted in a slightly longer distance covered – 7.5 miles in the hour. It felt good to stretch the legs and push the boundaries a bit more than last week.

Thursday:

An unusually long midweek bike session meant doing it in the early morning or at lunchtime was out of the question, and it was an evening date with the turbo trainer instead. Two hours on there with a faster-than-usual pace saw me clocking up an impressive 40 miles. Zipping along at 20mph, I couldn't help but wish I had chosen a flatter Ironman course. But then, where's the fun in that?

Friday:

Ah, Friday! The day of my now customary long run. Another three-hour session, pounding the pavement and canals in my steadfast heart-rate Zone 2. By now, I was pretty sure my Uber Eats driver thought I was either a professional athlete or just plain mad. Either way, I had become a familiar face, and my post-run dinner orders were probably the highlight of his evening. I crawled into bed this week; Ironman training and late nights were hitting me hard but the final long run was now in the bag.

Saturday:

My weekly pilgrimage to Media City for open-water swimming continued. Who knew how popular open-water swimming had become? There were definitely a few (more chiselled) triathletes there, but a bunch of old ladies, swimming in an impressively annoying four-person row, now needed to be swerved. This time, I clocked in at 1 hour and 3 minutes to cover 1.9 miles. I was tantalizingly close to the Ironman swim distance, and it got me daydreaming about the time I might post coming out of the water. Each stroke felt more confident, more assured – I was nearly there. My biggest fear, of looking a real tit on the day and not making the cut-off point – my Ironman dream over in 2 hours – now looked unfounded.

Sunday:

The final long ride before Ironman, and Coach Garrie's instructions were ringing in my ears. Despite the fatigue from the past two weeks, there was the same level of expectation: get back in the saddle and give me six hours! I managed to cover 90 miles, albeit with less than 4,000 feet of climbing. It's evident that the intensity of the previous sessions had caught up with me, but there was a sense of accomplishment in knowing that this was my last big ride before the big day.

As I wrapped up these two weeks of peak training, there was a mixed bag of emotions. There was the physical exhaustion, yes, but also a deep-seated satisfaction. The realisation that I was almost at the end of this gruelling training journey was both exhilarating and a tad bittersweet. The countdown to Ironman UK was in its final stretch, and I could almost taste the excitement in the air. Three weeks of tapering were now ahead of me, in some ways an attractive proposition, but, at the same time, a scary one. Now, it was very unlikely anything I did would lead to an improvement in my fitness. I had passed the time when it was recommended to try anything new, be it kit or nutrition. So, I was effectively done; all I had to do was get through the final few weeks injury free! Three weeks today, and it would be time. Bring it on, Ironman – I'm ready for you!

Bike setup, the rain is out, the mask is on. Bike envy kicked in.

T2 setup, I hoped to be back here in 24 hours after the bike route.

The night before. England top on, and tattoos have been applied.

The swim start ... we are nearly ready to go.

The Bolton Ironman course. Being out there for 8 hours, it could be quite a lonely, mentally taxing ride.

The finishing line in Bolton, on the steps of the town hall, the crowd in full flow.

For some it was a late night, with a 17-hour cut-off. The last people crossed the line just before midnight.

Hills, hills and more hills. With nearly 8,000 feet of elevation, Bolton Ironman bike course is one of the toughest.

Covid tests were required for every athlete this year, adding another treat to our races, a positive test.

The hill by the Black Dog pub. One of my favourite memories, and where Coach Garrie cheered us on.

The Ironman swim course – it was an intimidating beast, being in the middle of over 1,000 swimmers.

The famous Mexican wrestlers! This is what the Ironman is all about.

There are not many photos that show the extent to the rain – this is one of a few I found.

The Oompa Loompas! Not what I expected as I arrived at the first aid station

Chapter 33

Green Lights and Rule Books

After months of anticipation, with as many ups and downs as the proposed bike leg itself, the email finally landed in my inbox to confirm what us Ironman wannabes were hoping for: Ironman UK was a go! Cue the triumphant fanfare and a sigh of relief so loud it could've been heard in the next town. The WhatsApp group lit up with celebratory emojis and Max and I exchanged a virtual high-five.

The organisers, in a move as unexpected as finding a unicorn in your backyard, offered a 'swim-free' version of the event – a two-discipline option for those who felt deprived of pool time due to closures. But let's be real, after my new-found love affair with open-water swimming at Media City, skipping the swim was as likely as me turning down a post-race pizza. The thought was as fleeting as a British summer.

Along with this news, we were provided a link – a gentle nudge reminding us of the race day rules. It was like receiving the rules to the world's most strenuous board game, as every step, pedal and stride was governed by a handbook thicker than a triple-decker sandwich. With the physical torment of the training over, it was time to study up – race day was approaching, and it was all systems go!

Ah, the Ironman UK in Bolton – a battleground where dreams are forged, spirits are tested and a set of rules governs the chaos. Let's dive into the mystical rule book of this grand event, shall we? These are not a set of suggested guidelines open to interpretation. This is more like your school's stern headteacher laying down the law. The reality was, despite all your hard work, fall foul to any of these and your moment in the sun would be gone, and the Ironman medal would not be yours. Ironman is firm but fair, and the list of no-noes and restrictions are next level from your typical marathon race.

Rule 1: The Wetsuit Conundrum

In the world of Ironman, the wetsuit debate is akin to discussing the weather in Britain – you're never quite sure what you're going to get. The rule is simple: if the water is too warm, say goodbye to your beloved wetsuit. But let's be honest, we're in Bolton, not the Bahamas, so the chances of going 'au naturel' are slim. The likelihood of this being a non-wetsuit race was akin to Bolton Wanderers winning the Premier League sometime soon.

Rule 2: Drafting – The Forbidden Dance

Cycling in an Ironman is a bit like attending a school dance where the teachers have a zero-tolerance policy for getting too close. The no-drafting rule means keeping a 12m distance between you and the bike in front. Get too cosy, and you'll earn a penalty faster than you can say 'sorry, I just really liked the look of your bike!' This differs from most sportifs, where you will see groups of riders in a peloton, where riding in the belly of a pack is said to nearly double your energy savings by reducing aerodynamic drag. Rule 2 is a reminder that this is to be very much a solo endeavour.

Rule 3: The Great Transition

The transition areas in Ironman are less 'Cinderella' and more 'Cinderella with a stopwatch'. You're expected to switch from swim to bike, and bike to run with the efficiency of a Formula 1 pit stop. Dilly-dally, and you might as well bring out a picnic blanket. Crucially, avoiding indecent exposure may seem like an obvious rule, but faced with time restrictions and a wardrobe change required, it becomes more of a challenge. Indecent exposure and/or public nudity may result in a disqualification.

Rule 4: Nutrition – The DIY Project

You're expected to bring your own fuel for the day – gels, bars and whatever secret potion keeps you going, the exceptions being the onsite nutrition and any treats packed away in your special needs bag. Again, unlike your standard marathon, if an official sees you taking a harmless jelly baby from a spectator, you're done for. No outside help is allowed, no matter how small it seems. Just remember, littering is also a big no-no. Drop a gel wrapper, and you are risking that much-coveted finisher's medal.

Rule 5: The Attire

In the fashion-forward world of Ironman, there's a strict dress code. Wetsuits must be of a certain thickness and shoes must be strapped in before mounting your bike. Don't dream of touching your bike at all until your helmet is on your head and fastened – yes Ironman is very safety conscious and strict.

Rule 6: The Gadgets

Oh, the gadgets! Heart-rate monitors, GPS watches, power meters – Ironman UK is in one way a mobile exhibition for tech lovers. But be warned: headphones are a big no. That's right, it doesn't matter if you are out there for the full 17 hours – no music allowed, boyo. As for mobile phones – forget it. You'll need to hum your motivational tunes for this race.

Rule 7: Bow to the Officials

In the regal court of Ironman UK, the race officials are akin to the Queen's Guard – stoic, observant and not to be trifled with. Respecting these noble sentinels of the race is paramount. They're the ones who ensure that the Ironman kingdom runs smoothly, and their word is law. Argue with an official, and you might find yourself banished from the realm (or at least serving a time penalty in the naughty corner). Jokes aside, these naughty corners do exist. Break any rules included here, and even if not severe enough for them to remove you from the race, you will be locked into the next transitional section until you have served your time penalty, those precious race minutes helplessly passing you by.

Rule 8: Beat the Clock or Face the Chopping Block

Ah, the cut-off times – Ironman UK's version of Cinderella's midnight curfew. These are non-negotiable deadlines that each athlete must meet at various stages of the race and probably the biggest difference from your standard marathon. Most marathons, for their merit, are built to be truly inclusive affairs. It doesn't matter if you are chasing a Boston qualifying time or chugging along for a six-hour finish, both are treated as finishers and go home with their medals around their necks. Not at Ironman: this race is built differently. There are cut-offs throughout the race (more on this to come) leading to a final time of 17 hours to complete the course. You can be Lance Armstrong on the bike and Eliud Kipchoge on the run, but take 2 hours 30 mins to complete the swim and you won't be given the chance to show the world. It's a race against time, literally. So, if you find yourself dilly-dallying at an aid station, remember: the clock is ticking, and Father Time waits for no one in an Ironman.

Rule 9: Lone Wolf Syndrome – No Outside Assistance

In the world of Ironman, it's every athlete for themselves. The rule of no outside assistance is like being in a spy movie – you're on a solo mission, and the only help you get is from official aid stations. This means no sneaky energy gels from a spouse, no magical bike repairs from a friend, and certainly no comfort food handed over from your mum at the halfway point. It's you, your gear and your wits against the course. This may sound a done deal, but try dealing with a flat tyre 100 miles into a cycle ride, shivering and energy-sapped. The support of friends, family and even strangers may have got you here, but that ends now. Think of it as a test of your resourcefulness, of planning for every occasion; a trial by fire, or in this case by water, wheels and weary legs.

Rule 10: The Finish Line Etiquette

Crossing the finish line is a moment of glory, but remember, it's not the Oscars. That means, however emotional it is, it is you alone who crosses the line. Unlike other rival triathlon companies, that means no holding your child, your other half or that dog that's kept you company on all the long runs. No one wants to have completed 140.6 miles only to be banished for a rule-break at the finishing line. Accept your medal gracefully, try not to trip over the red carpet, and save the tears for when you find your loved ones – or the nearest massage tent.

In conclusion, the rules of Ironman UK in Bolton are a unique blend of strict guidelines, survival tactics and a test of one's ability to adapt and overcome. It's a journey through the beautiful English countryside, peppered with rules that add to the adventure. Are these rules hard? Yes. A little harsh? Maybe. But Ironman is not set up to be an easy race. It is a solo mission that is designed to test even the fittest. Good luck, and may the rules be ever in your favour!

Chapter 34
The Taper – Embracing the Calm Before the Storm

As the taper period began, I found myself in a peculiar mental state. On one side, I was so close to the end of this roller-coaster journey, and after months of intensity a lighter training load awaited. On the negative, I had felt like a tiny raft floating towards a looming waterfall edge, blissfully unaware of the dangers that were fast approaching. Then as the physical load eased, it allowed my active mind to focus on all the threats that could potentially derail my grand plans for Ironman. For months, I had trained with the steadfast belief that Ironman UK would happen. Every stroke, pedal and stride had been a step towards that goal. But it was impossible to squash those pesky what-ifs lurking in the back of my mind. The swim, in particular, had been a nerve-wracking roller coaster – a waiting game for pools to open, followed by a frantic dash to get race-ready. Then there was the bike debacle, where my trusty steed almost turned into my Achilles heel, only to be saved by the true hero of this story, my local mechanic. And let's not forget the looming spectre of race cancellations, which threatened to relegate my Ironman dreams to a future date, when I would be filled with sleep deprivation and a constant aroma of nappies.

Now, what's this tapering business, you ask? Well, it's essentially the triathlon equivalent of slowing down to enjoy the scenery. It's a period of reduced training volume and intensity, recommended by coaches to let your body recuperate and be in peak condition going in to race day. Think of it as easing off the pedal to arrive at your destination in tip-top shape, rather than careening into it like a runaway train, aka my last Ironman training debacle.

The taper lasted three weeks. Coach Garrie, in his infinite wisdom, methodically reduced my training load by around two hours each week. The sessions still packed a punch but lacked the previous weeks' relentless intensity. And yes, there was still a cheeky 15-mile run nestled in there, but after the mayhem of the previous months, it allowed for a taste of normality where my schedule could fit in a few more social occasions and less Lycra.

But with this decrease in physical exertion came an increase in mental gymnastics. The countdown to race day was now measured in days, not weeks. Bloody hell. It seemed just days ago this 4 July was an almost mythical date in the future; now it was very real. The anticipation was palpable, a mix of excitement and nerves. Would all the training pay off? Could I translate months of discipline and dedication into a successful race day?

Then it began, like the different stages of grief: I went through a spectrum of emotional stages.

Stage One: The Sweet Relief

The initial phase of the taper was a soothing feeling to both body and mind. After eight gruelling months, the notion that the hardest work was behind me was comforting. Coach Garrie's mantra was simple: 'You've done the hard yards, now it's time to let the body and mind recuperate.' He explained, much to my relief, that no matter how hard I pushed in these final weeks, the science indicated no significant gains in fitness would be made. This period was about maintenance, keeping the ship steady as it approached the harbour. No more, no less than what he prescribed – don't be tempted to push it.

A new swear rule was introduced during this phase by Coach Garrie: 'new' became a three-letter word not to be muttered under any circumstances. This meant no new gear, no experimental tech and certainly no novel nutrition tricks despite any unbelievable promises of improved race-day performance. My kit for race day needed to be decided now and tested in every session possible (and as fast as my washing machine could return it). This rule, strangely, was a source of comfort. It removed the temptation to throw a last-minute curveball into my plans, and was also a relief to my wallet.

Stage Two: The Dawning Reality

As the taper progressed, the enormity of the upcoming challenge dawned on me. All the training, the virtual loops, the on-course training weekends – they had all been leading to this. Now, the focus shifted to logistics, the nitty-gritty of race-day preparations that went beyond physical training. The rule book wasn't just a set of guidelines, it was another mental challenge, something that needed to be learned; no excuses would be allowed by officials on race day.

Then came the calls – to friends and family, recruiting a support crew for the big day. The realisation hit me hard; this wasn't just about me and my pregnant cheerleader, Briony. The scale of the event demanded a team, a band of helpers to navigate the logistical labyrinth of Ironman UK. Briony had been amazing, but as her bump became more prominent, the thought of leaving her in crowds alone made me nervous, and to ask her to navigate what promised to be a 20-hour day, from the starting point, to picking a weary Ironman husband up at the finishing line, then helping recover bags and my bike, would be a step too far. Reinforcements would be needed.

Stage Three: The Paranoia Strikes

Despite eight months of training, with barely a niggle or an illness in sight, in the final leg of the taper, my body seemed to turn into a drama queen, throwing up all sorts of imaginary ailments. First, there was the phantom foot injury

– a sudden, unexplained pain in the arch of my foot that sent me into a spiral of anxiety. A frantic call to Coach Garrie resulted in an immediate holt for the remaining planned runs, a decision that felt both wise and in hindsight was slightly overcautious.

Then there was the cough – a small, seemingly innocuous thing that became the focus of my heightened paranoia. The spectre of Covid-19, which had loomed large over the past year, suddenly felt all too real. Memories of my battle with pneumonia resurfaced, fuelling my fears. Could this be it? Could a virus derail my Ironman dream at the 11th hour for the second time in a row?

These final weeks of the taper were a roller coaster of emotions. The physical strain of training was replaced by a mental tug-of-war. Every day brought a new challenge, a fresh wave of doubts and fears. But amidst this was a glimmer of excitement, a flicker of anticipation for what was to come. The thought of that finishing line brought a smile, before I checked myself with a reminder not to get ahead of the game.

As Ironman UK inched closer, my paranoia about every conceivable disaster that could derail my race reached its peak. Sensing my growing anxiety, my two best mates from school, Craig and Gary (not to be confused with Coach Garrie), decided to stage an intervention. They whisked me away for a day of light-hearted fun – a day of foot golf (for the uninitiated, a strange combo of football and golf, think bigger balls and fewer clubs) followed by a pub lunch. It was a well-needed distraction, a day to remind me there was a world beyond Ironman training.

Our friendship, though somewhat neglected over the past year due to family commitments, Covid restrictions and my training schedule, hadn't changed one jot. As we joked and laughed on the course, it felt like we were back in secondary school, without a care in the world. For the first time in weeks I was laughing and joking. I was atrociously bad at foot golf, trailing behind Craig and Gary, but I didn't mind. I even managed to suppress the irrational fear of pulling a hamstring as I kicked the ball around.

Returning home, Briony noticed the change in me immediately. The usual pre-race irritability, exacerbated by the looming shadow of Ironman, had lifted slightly. The day out with Craig and Gary had worked wonders, injecting a dose of normality into my taper-crazed life. I owed them a lot that day; the release of pressure had done me the world of good.

Now, all that was left to do was wait. The training was done, my gear was prepped and, miraculously, I had evaded injuries and illnesses. The final week before Ironman UK was upon me, a week filled with a mix of anticipation, nerves and a strange sense of calm. What would be, would be. I could do no more.

In the final days leading to 4 July, I found myself reflecting on this journey I had been on. The early mornings, the gruelling training sessions, the sacrifices – they had all led to this. I was hopefully on the cusp of achieving something I had once thought impossible. As I had lain in that hospital bed, pneumonia plaguing my lungs, the beeping of the machines and the rain hitting the windows, I had felt embarrassed and broken. No matter what would happen next Sunday in the race itself, I would now make it there – of that I was sure – and that made this Ironman a hell of a lot better than the last one.

The final piece of my prep now remained. A pre-race preparation call with my guide for this journey, Coach Garrie. This wasn't just any call; it was *the* call – the final strategy session before the big day arrived.

Chapter 35
The Final Zoom and the Race-day Strategy

There I was, perched in front of my laptop, ready for my final Zoom call with Coach Garrie before I would see him in Bolton in just a few short days. This wasn't just any call; it was the ultimate pre-game pep talk, the last nugget of wisdom before I plunged into the Ironman abyss. We were about to dissect the course, strategise and basically ensure I didn't turn into a headless chicken come race day.

We dived straight into discussing the swim in the now somewhat familiar waters of Pennington Flash, nestled 11 miles south of Bolton. Here, I was to conquer two laps to hit the mystical 2.4-mile mark of the Ironman swim. Ah, the swim – my once-nemesis turned uneasy ally. My biggest fear? The notorious 'washing machine effect' at the start of the swim, where arms and legs churn the water into a frothy frenzy, resembling a particularly aggressive laundry day. It's not uncommon for an Ironman novice to be pulled from the water, panicked after receiving a rogue arm and kick to the face.

Coach Garrie advised me that the water in Pennington Flash wouldn't be as refined as Salford Quays, but at least I wouldn't have to battle waves or currents like some sea-based Ironman events. The water temperature was looking to be around 19°C – chilly, but nothing a bit of neoprene couldn't handle. I planned to don my extra neoprene cap underneath the mandatory Ironman swim cap for good measure.

The swim was set to start between 6 and 6:30am, with athletes self-seeding based on their expected finish time. The cut-off time was 2 hours and 20 minutes. Garrie inquired about my target. Flashbacks of my early open-water escapades, where I had resembled a panicked dog more than a swimmer, and had just hoped to finish under the cut-off. Now though, with every passing week, my form and time had improved. 'Best case, around 1 hour 20 minutes, but anything under 1 hour 30 minutes would be grand,' I replied, with cautious optimism.

Coach Garrie's advice was to seed myself with the 1 hour 25-minute group. His reasoning was sound – it would minimise the risk of being bulldozed by faster swimmers yet avoid getting bogged down by a slower crowd that would block my path. He suggested aiming to position myself just right of the direct route once in the water. It was a strategic move, adding negligible time but offering a clearer path and potentially less chaos. 'Think of it as taking the scenic route, just with less scenery and just a little less splashing,' he quipped.

As the call progressed, we discussed the nuances of the swim – sighting landmarks, pacing and the all-important exit strategy. 'Remember, getting out of the water is just as important as getting in. You don't want to be the guy who celebrates finishing the swim, only to trip over his own feet, ending your Ironman there,' Garrie warned, only half-joking.

With the swim strategy tucked neatly under our belts, Coach Garrie and I moved on to the next Herculean task of the Ironman challenge – the 112-mile bike assault. After a quick Superman-style change in Transition 1, I planned to refuel and launch on to the bike, ready to face the day's main course.

The bike leg starts with an appetiser – an eight-mile-odd cycle from Pennington Flash, before joining the main course at Chorley New Road. This bit was the only part of the course I hadn't experienced yet, but it looked 'relatively' flat, so I hoped to maintain a decent speed in order to bank some time. From there, I'd embark on three laps that would dominate the bulk of my day. The course meanders east towards Bury, then north through Edgeworth, where the real scenic, thigh-burning journey begins. We're talking about a picturesque but punishing ride through Lancashire's countryside, culminating in the infamous Sheephouse Lane, before swooping down Chorley New Road and looping back to Queens Park for laps two and three. The total ascent? A mere 8,000 feet – just a Sunday stroll, if your idea of a stroll involves scaling small mountains on two wheels.

Thanks to my virtual training sessions on Rouvy, I felt intimately acquainted with the route. Coach Garrie inquired about my approach, and I laid out my game plan. The route was mentally dissected into three major climbs per lap. I was as ready for them as one could be, armed with Coach Garrie's advice to control my heart rate, resist the urge to power up the hills like a Tour de France wannabe and remember the small detail of a marathon still waiting for me. Controlling heart rates and energy levels was going to be key.

The cumbersome, top-heavy water system of my first loop attempt was long out of the picture. My hydration strategy was simple – two water bottles, one filled with water, the other with a carb drink, complemented by a fuel pouch stuffed with gels, bananas and replacement carb drink sachets. I had a strict schedule for consuming each, aiming to keep my energy levels as optimally topped-up as a high-end smartphone.

Then came the all-important discussion about timings. The total cut-off time for the bike segment was 10 hours and 30 minutes from the start of the swim. Worst case scenario: if I took 2 hours and 20 minutes for the swim and ten minutes in T1, that left me with eight hours for the bike. However, I was hoping to bank some extra time in the swim and I knew I could do with that buffer. My times on the virtual course had been improving steadily, and my best-case scenario for the bike was around seven hours. But factoring in those extra miles, real-world fatigue and a healthy dose of caution, I was targeting around eight hours. Any longer, and I'd need a stellar swim to keep me out of the dreaded DNF territory.

I felt a mixture of excitement and a healthy respect for the bike challenge ahead. The bike leg was not just a test of endurance but a balancing act of strategy, nutrition, and mental fortitude. It was about pedalling through the pain, the hills and the inevitable moments of doubt. But armed with my plan and Garrie's guidance, I felt ready. The hills of Lancashire awaited, and I was prepared to conquer them – one pedal stroke at a time. Ironman UK, bring on your bike course; I'm ready to roll! Let's just hope I could stay puncture-free!

Coach Garrie then shifted the conversation to the final leg of this Ironman triathlon – the run. This wasn't just any run, it was a marathon after an already gruelling swim and bike ride, so previous marathon times were out the window. The route would take me from Transition 2 at Queens Park into the heart of Bolton. I'd be passing along Bark Street and Knowsley Street, turning around Victoria Square, with the Town Hall teasingly in sight – a constant reminder of the finish line that was so close yet so far. Each of the four laps included a nasty incline through Queens Park, adding up to a total elevation gain of 1,250 feet in total. At the end of each lap, I would be given a different-coloured band – a rainbow of suffering that marked my progress, or served as a vivid reminder of how much further I had to go.

I confessed to Coach Garrie that, assuming I made it through the swim and bike unscathed and injury-free, I felt cautiously optimistic about the run. The final cut-off time was 17 hours from the start, giving me, in the worst-case scenario, about 6 hours and 30 minutes to complete the marathon. Under normal circumstances, this would be completely feasible, not even a consideration. However, Garrie was quick to remind me that this was far from normal. The swim, the cycle, the hills – nothing about the Ironman shout be taken for granted or treated lightly.

We then discussed my gel strategy for the run, making sure I had a plan for consistent energy replenishment. But more importantly, Garrie emphasised the need to walk up the hill in Queens Park each lap. 'Your ego might want to sprint up that hill, but remember, you're in this to finish, not qualify for the world championships,' he advised. He suggested considering a run-walk strategy, especially if my energy started to wane. 'Conserve your energy, keep an eye on your heart rate and, for heaven's sake, don't forget to eat and drink,' Coach Garrie added.

The idea of walking part of the marathon initially bruised my ego. I had always imagined myself running triumphantly through the entire course, smashing my and Coach Garrie's expectations in a blaze of glory. But Coach Garrie's advice was grounded in reality – this was about endurance, about making it to the finish line in one piece. This was a marathon, not a sprint, in the most literal sense. I was here to complete, not to compete.

The strategy was set – swim, bike and run (with a bit of walking) my way to the end of Ironman UK. The training was done, the plan was in place, and all that was left was to execute it. As I hung up the call and closed the laptop, I felt a sense of calm. I was ready for this – ready to face the final challenge, ready to complete my Ironman journey. Bolton, here I come – with a solid plan, a strong heart and a pair of tired but determined legs.

Chapter 36
The Pre-Race Set-up – A Sunny Calm Before the Storm

On Friday, 2 July, two days before the big event, I woke up to a storm brewing – but unfortunately for me it was not a theoretical but a literal storm. My phone was buzzing with notifications from the Ironman WhatsApp group, filled with weather reports predicting everything from wind and rain to potential thunderstorms. It seemed like Mother Nature was having a bit of a mood swing, and the chances of a dry, sunny Sunday were looking as slim as my odds of taking home the Ironman trophy and a qualification spot for the Ironman World Championships in Kona.

That day marked the beginning of my Ironman race weekend. After the best part of a year of talking and training, everything was about to become a lot more tangible and ... well ... real, as we would travel to Bolton to set up and complete the pre-race formalities. We were also preparing for a much-needed week of rest and recovery down at Briony's family home in Cornwall. That would be my chosen location to celebrate and recover or, if circumstances did not go my way, to commiserate and hide away.

Briony and I set off for Bolton to embark on the sacred ritual of registration. Arriving at Queens Park, the weather was playing a cruel joke on us. There I was, clad in shorts, a T-shirt and sunglasses, in what would have been perfect conditions for a leisurely run around Bolton – a stark contrast to the ominous forecast for race day itself.

Due to Covid-19 restrictions, Briony had to wait outside the main tent. Masked up, I entered at my pre-booked time slot, feeling a mix of excitement and nerves. The registration process was seamless – a well-oiled machine as you'd expect from an organisation like Ironman. As I registered,

I received the customary Ironman swag – a large blue backpack that seemed not only waterproof but also capable of the important job of announcing to the world that I was an Ironman competitor (and hopefully, soon-to-be finisher). The backpack was followed by an Ironman wristband and final instructions for the big day itself. Remembering Coach Garrie's advice from the training weekend, I made a beeline to request the special needs bags.

Registration complete and bags in hand, next up was the adjoining merchandise shop – oh, the temptation! The array of Ironman-branded gear could have easily lightened my wallet considerably. There was no doubt about it – I wanted it all, be it the mugs, the T-shirts, the hats, the commemorative race socks ... This all seemed crucial in my new-found understanding that once you have completed an Ironman, you must take every opportunity to tell the world you have completed an Ironman. But a part of me hesitated, not wanting to jinx Sunday's outcome. Investing heavily in Ironman merch before crossing the finish line felt like counting my chickens before they hatched.

After resisting the lure of the merchandise, I had a chance to regroup with Briony and I collected a few samples from the various stalls outside – gels, beer, and other freebies from official suppliers. We took a stroll around, absorbing the atmosphere, the buzz of anticipation. We gazed over at T2, which now felt incredibly real. This was the spot where I hoped to be dropping off my bike in just over 48 hours, gearing up for the marathon leg of the race.

The day wouldn't be complete without the obligatory mini photoshoot in front of the Ironman branded truck. There we were, Briony and I, smiling for the camera, Ironman backpack in tow, capturing the moment before the storm – both literal and metaphorical. It was a surreal feeling that after months of preparation, I was standing

TRI AGAIN

there, on the cusp of what would be one of the biggest challenges of my life.

We did, however, save the best to last. We walked the five minutes or so to Bolton town centre, and to the intimidating town hall. At the bottom of the steps was what I wanted to see ... the famous Ironman finisher chute, with the finish line erect and the red carpet that led the way under it. A quick picture was taken and sent to Max; this was what we had dreamed of for the past eight months. Hopefully we'd both be seeing it again in less than 48 hours' time.

As we left Bolton town centre, the air was thick with anticipation and a hint of nervous energy. The set-up day had been a mix of practicalities, excitement and a little bit of merch-induced temptation. But more than anything, it was the day when the Ironman UK ceased to be an abstract concept in my training schedule and transformed into a tangible, imminent reality. Ironman was well and truly in town.

Saturday morning dawned, a stark contrast to the previous day's sunny disposition. It was as if I had woken up in a different world – one where the sky was a canvas of ominous grey, streaked with rain clouds ready to burst. Today was the day for bike and bag drop-offs, and the weather seemed intent on making it as memorable (and challenging) as possible.

Coach Garrie's instructions for the day were clear and unequivocal: get the drop-offs done early, then head home and spend as much time off my feet as possible, saving as much physical and mental energy as I could for the next day. A simple enough plan, but as we drove to Pennington Flash, the home of Transition 1, the relentless rain made it feel like a mission.

Pennington Flash, the very spot where I would emerge from the water tomorrow, transition from swim to bike, felt different under the grey, rain-laden sky. It was here that I had to leave my trusty Boardman bike, along with all my cycling gear for T1. As we arrived, the heavens opened, unleashing a downpour.

The first order of business upon entering the transition area was a mandatory bike check. Brakes, gears, general functionality – everything was scrutinised by the officials on entry, a process that felt even more vital given the foreboding weather warnings. Once cleared, I racked my bike in its designated spot. That's when the imposter syndrome really hit me.

Surrounded by sleek, carbon-fibre cycling machines that looked like they cost more than the car we'd arrived in and were designed to devour the Bolton hills, my Boardman suddenly seemed quaint, almost out of place. But as Coach Garrie had advised, I shrugged off the intimidation, covered my bike with a plastic cover to shield it from the elements, and moved on to the next task.

Helmet positioned, shoes laid out, nutrition strategically placed, I went through the motions, setting up my T1 with meticulous care. Then it was off to the tent to hang up my bag containing my post-swim essentials – clothes, towel and additional nutrition.

Briony and I then took a walk to the water's edge. The poor visibility could not conceal the size of the task. Despite the terrible weather in the distance, I could still see the buoys, adorned with Ironman flags, bobbing ominously in the water. In less than 24 hours, I'd be in there, amidst those choppy waters, swimming the required 2.4 miles. The reality of the challenge I was about to face hit me anew. But the swim, which had once been my greatest fear, now felt like an old adversary I was ready to confront.

The final act of the day led me back to Queens Park, this time to T2 – the second transition area. In less than 24 hours, the place had transformed from a sunny, serene set-up spot into a bustling beehive of activity under a canopy of murky clouds. The previously calm atmosphere had been replaced by a tangible buzz of anticipation and, dare I say, a touch of pre-race jitters.

The park was swarming with athletes, a parade of lean, focused figures, each absorbed in their own pre-race rituals. The air was thick with a blend of excitement and anxiety, as if the weather had decided to mirror the collective mood of the participants. Everyone seemed to be on a mission, moving with a purpose that only those about to embark on an Ironman could understand.

Compared to the leisurely pace of yesterday's registration, today was a whirlwind. I made my way to the T2 tent, a structure that had sprung up overnight, ready to play a pivotal role in tomorrow's event. Inside, I found my designated spot and hung up my bag, now filled with the gear for the final leg of the race – running clothes, shoes and an arsenal of gels. This bag held the essentials for the marathon that awaited me after the gruelling bike ride. It felt surreal to be preparing for something so monumental, yet here I was, hanging up a bag with the calmness of someone packing for a leisurely jog.

Once my T2 duties were fulfilled, it was time to heed Coach Garrie's advice – to rest and conserve energy for the mammoth day ahead. Leaving the bustling scene at Queens Park, I couldn't help but feel a pang of excitement mixed with nerves. The transformation of Bolton into an Ironman hub was complete, and the reality of what was to come was hitting me full force.

The rest of the afternoon was spent in a strange limbo, a mix of trying to relax and the growing anticipation of the race ahead. Every now and then, I'd catch myself staring at the ceiling, lost in thoughts of the swim, bike and run that lay ahead. The quiet before the storm was both a blessing and a curse – a chance to gather my thoughts, but also a little too much time to overthink.

Chapter 37

The Eve of Ironman – A Night of Calm, Carbs and Football

The night before the Ironman, Craig, my footgolf compadre, school friend and the appointed sherpa for the weekend, arrived, ready to play his part in the grand adventure. Leaving his family behind for a couple of days, Craig, a burly tree surgeon with a physique that screamed 'lumberjack', was the perfect person for the job. His role? To get me to the start line in one piece and then switch to being Briony's support crew as she navigated the chaos of race day, heavily pregnant and, understandably, not as mobile as before.

As we briefed Craig on the day's plan, he listened with a mix of amusement and bewilderment. The world of triathlons was as foreign to him as his weights regime was to me. We agreed that it would be futile for him and Briony to try to spot me during the bike leg. Instead, they'd head home for some rest and return to catch me during the marathon stage. Craig was not only the brawn needed for post-race bike logistics but, as a bonus, his truck – a vehicle so large it could probably transport a small forest (and during the week likely did) – was ideal for hauling my gear home after the day's events.

The evening brought a final message from Coach Garrie, his words a blend of encouragement and sage advice. He urged me to stay positive, to trust in the months of training that had led me to this point. 'Remember the triumphs, not the hiccups,' he said, reminding me not to dwell on the occasional missed session. His parting wisdom was to savour the experience – this was my moment in the spotlight, the culmination of all those early mornings and late nights. And, in true Coach Garrie style, he threw in one last practical tip: 'Wipe your nose before crossing the finish line. You don't want your moment of glory captured with your face marred by a snot!' If ever there was advice that proved his years of experience training people like me for this event, this was it!

The Ironman WhatsApp group was buzzing with activity, a digital hub of nervous energy and excitement. My phone was lighting up like the Blackpool illuminations with each new message. Selfies of athletes at registration, pictures of meticulously set-up bikes, and last-minute queries from nervous first-timers filled the chat. The group atmosphere was obviously electric ahead of the biggest day in most of their race calendars.

Amongst the flurry of messages, there were reassuring words from the veterans of the group. Their advice was a blend of humour and wisdom, typical of people who had faced the Ironman beast before. One message stood out for its blunt simplicity: 'Don't be shit.' It made me chuckle – a perfect summary of the unspoken Ironman mantra. I sent out a round of good luck wishes, knowing I'd likely see some of these faces tomorrow, either at the start line or on the sidelines along the course. Some others who were taking part in the event, I may even see out there.

The final message of the night was a video from Max, my virtual training buddy and unexpected ally on this journey. His face filled the screen, his newly acquired Bolton Ironman hat perched proudly on his head, clearly freshly purchased from the merchandise tent. His message was a mix of encouragement and humour, his daughter chiming in with her own adorable rendition of 'good luck'. It was a heartfelt moment from someone who, just eight months ago, had been a stranger. Now, here he was, an integral part of my Ironman journey, offering support and camaraderie from afar.

Eager to stop my mind overthinking, I made a few quick calls to my family and some friends. It was a set of brief but comforting conversations, filled with encouragement and last-minute well-wishes but I was too distracted to offer any great value to any of the conversations. Afterwards, I put my phone away, determined to give my eyes (and mind) a break from the incessant glow of the screen. Tonight, rest was my priority, and I intended to do everything possible to ensure a good night's sleep.

My last pre-race task was somewhat nostalgic – applying temporary tattoos to my arm. Provided at registration, these weren't the whimsical designs of childhood but rather my race number, '1168'. As I carefully placed the numbers on my arm, I couldn't help but feel like a kid again, albeit with a far more serious purpose. These numbers were my identifier, particularly crucial in the swim where traditional race bibs were impractical. If anything went awry, especially in the water, these numbers were my lifeline, ensuring I could be quickly identified.

Dinner was a culinary triumph courtesy of Briony – a carb-lover's dream of fresh garlic bread and pasta, perfectly balanced to be stomach-friendly yet energy-packed ahead of a full day's racing. Craig, ever the good sport, was cheerful as he grilled us on tomorrow's events and plans for the new baby, due in three months, as we indulged in the hearty meal, fuelling up for the monumental day ahead.

Post-dinner, it was time for a dose of normality – the Euro 2020 quarter-final football match between England and Ukraine. Under usual circumstances, Craig and I would have been amidst a boisterous crowd in a local pub, soaking in the excitement. But tonight the setting was far more subdued, our eyes glued to the TV in the living room. All I hoped for was a swift conclusion to the match – extra time was not on my pre-Ironman agenda.

As we settled in to watch the game, I treated myself to one non-alcoholic beer. England vs Ukraine, a match charged with high stakes and higher hopes. The game unfolded with

England displaying a dominating performance. Much to my relief, the match was far from the nail-biter many had anticipated, turning into a display of England's prowess on the field. With every goal, the prospect of extra time dwindled. There was to be no nerve-shredding display like England typically produced. It seemed like the football and Ironman gods had aligned this year. The final whistle blew and England had secured a place in the semi-finals against Denmark with a resounding 4-0 victory. The excitement of the win was a welcome distraction, a momentary escape from the nerves of the upcoming race. The question was, by the time England kicked off against Denmark midweek, would I officially be an Ironman or licking my wounds?

As the post-match interviews got underway, I realised that despite this being a welcome distraction, it was time to focus back on the mission ahead. While half of the country would drink late into the evening and early morning celebrating this victory, I had other plans. I thanked Craig and Briony for their support and company, feeling a strange sense of calm amidst the pre-race jitters. The day had been a blend of final preparations, heartfelt conversations and a brief escape into the world of football.

I excused myself, aware that every minute of sleep was precious. I headed to bed, the reality of what awaited me in the morning looming large. The Ironman challenge was no longer a distant dream; it was mere hours away. The training, the sacrifices, the early mornings and late nights – it was all leading to this.

At a speed that would have made for a great transition time, I was upstairs, teeth cleaned and in bed just moments later, my wetsuit and warm clothing poised ready at the end of my bed. Lying there, I breathed deeply, allowing myself a moment to reflect on the journey. My mind was a mixture of excitement, nerves and anticipation – it all swirled around as I drifted towards sleep. Tomorrow was finally the day of the Ironman, when I would face the biggest physical and mental challenge of my life. As I closed my eyes, I embraced the uncertainty, the excitement and the sheer scale of the adventure that awaited.

Ironman UK, I thought to myself as sleep finally enveloped me, let's see what you've got. I'm ready for you.

Part 4: The Race

Chapter 38

Dawn of the Ironman – A Blend of Oats, Nerves and Neoprene

The alarm buzzed mercilessly at 4am, a clear reminder that the day I had been training for was no longer a distant dream but a glaring reality. Groggily, I wolfed down my carefully planned double portion of oats, dark chocolate and peanut butter. It was a meal meant for energy, but at this ungodly hour it was more a test of willpower than a breakfast of champions.

Clad in my wetsuit, topped with a hoodie for warmth, I joined Craig, Briony (and the ever-present bump) in the pickup truck. We drove the 20-odd miles to Pennington Flash and the roads were eerily quiet, as expected at 4:30am on a Sunday. That tranquillity, however, was short-lived: as we neared Pennington, a traffic jam of athletes and their supporters emerged, a convoy of nervous excitement heading towards the same destination.

We followed the recommendations and parked up at the nearby Leigh Sports Village. The car park was a sea of athletes in neoprene wetsuits, their faces a mix of determination and pre-race jitters. Supporters mingled among them, offering last-minute pep talks and words of encouragement. Without needing directions, we simply joined the flow of people heading towards the Flash, a procession of triathlon pilgrims making their way to the waterside.

Arriving at Pennington Flash, the earlier concerns about the weather seemed unfounded. The waters lay calm, with just a hint of mist hovering above the surface – almost idyllic race conditions. But there was no time to admire the scenery. I had a few pre-race tasks to attend to, starting with dropping off my streetwear clothing bag – the set of clothes I hoped to don post-race, assuming all went well.

Next, it was time to give the Boardman one last check. The plastic cover, which had shielded it from the overnight rain, came off, revealing my faithful steed. A quick pump of the tyres and a brief once-over ensured everything was race-ready. I mounted my bike computer in readiness, positioned my gels and patted it goodbye, hopeful of a reunion in a couple of hours. It was a moment of quiet connection with my bike, a silent pep talk before the long journey ahead.

As I finished up with my bike, the reality of the day ahead hit me. The swim in Pennington Flash, the bike leg through the Lancashire countryside, the marathon through Bolton – it was all about to start.

Sensing nerves, Craig clapped a reassuring hand on my shoulder. Craig's expression was a mix of pride and bemusement about what he could see in front of him: a very different proposition to his typical morning regime in the gym. Briony, managing her own excitement and the demands of being six months pregnant, offered a smile that was both encouraging and slightly apprehensive. They both knew what it had taken to get there. Briony had especially seen me at my lowest of lows, hospital-bound and gasping for air, so she knew this was my shot at redemption and we all just prayed it would happen today.

Following Ironman's recommendation to arrive 90 minutes before the start proved conservative and we found ourselves with time to spare after smoothly completing the bag drop and bike check. The area around Pennington Flash had transformed into a mini carnival of sorts, complete with booming music and an undeniable buzz of excitement in the air. Athletes and supporters mingled, their faces a mix of nerves and anticipation, all set against the backdrop of an emerging dawn.

We wandered around for a bit, soaking in the atmosphere of the big day. The energy was infectious and for non-competitors it would have been an amazing occasion, but as the minutes ticked by I found myself craving a bit of tranquillity amidst the chaos. The crowd was exhilarating but overwhelming and I longed for a quieter space to gather my thoughts.

Briony and Craig didn't need to be told this, they could sense it in my body language, and spotted a small cove slightly removed from the bustling throng of people. It seemed we weren't the only ones seeking refuge; a few pro athletes and their coaches had also congregated there, a testament to their experience in navigating the pre-race landscape.

In our new-found haven, we took a few moments to relax. We snapped some pictures, capturing the calm before the storm. I pointed out to Briony and Craig what I believed to be the turning buoy in the distance, marking the corner of the triangular swim course.

The conversation then turned to the logistics of spotting me in the water. Craig, in his typical fashion, wondered aloud how they'd be able to pick me out among the sea of athletes, all clad in mandatory black wetsuits and identical pale blue swim caps. Briony chimed in with a laugh, assuring him that I'd be easy to spot thanks to my 'unique' swimming style – a comment that was both amusing and slightly unnerving as I contemplated the impending swim. It wasn't exactly the pep talk I required at the time! (Note: Briony stands by this statement to this day, claiming that's how she spotted me. I still do not know what makes my technique and stroke so unique, and feel slightly cheated after so many hours purposely teaching myself a very particular swimming style!)

As we chatted, the speakers nearby played an eclectic mix of music, setting the tone for the day. One song in particular really hit me – 'One Day Like This' by Elbow. I'd never paid much attention to the song before, never a fan of Elbow, but in that moment it resonated deeply, shifting my nervous energy to a more grounded state. The lyrics seemed to echo the sentiment of the day, a reminder to seize the moment and embrace the experience.

Surrounded by the serene setting of our little cove, with the comforting presence of Briony and Craig, and the uplifting soundtrack provided by the event organisers, I felt a sense of peace wash over me.

As we made our way back to the main area, the first hints of sunrise began to paint the sky, casting a gentle light over Pennington Flash. The Ironman UK was about to begin, and I was as ready as I could ever be. Let's do this – one day like this, a day to remember.

I caught sight of Coach Garrie and a few other familiar faces from the training weekend. They were perched atop one of the picnic tables, a spot typically reserved for leisurely Sunday family outings, now transformed into a vantage point for coaches to survey the sea of athletes. We exchanged brief greetings and waves, but the growing buzz and limited space allowed for little more than that.

As per the plan discussed with Coach Garrie, I positioned myself among the group of swimmers aiming for a 1 hour 25 minute completion time. The mandatory face masks we all wore created a surreal scene – a sea of masked athletes, all mentally preparing for the imminent swim. Among the crowd, I bumped into a few acquaintances from the training weekend. We exchanged quick words of encouragement, a few fist bumps, a shared understanding of the journey that had brought us here.

Standing there, I was struck by an observation that I had been warned by Coach Garrie would happen. There I was, barely 5ft 8in in stature and everyone around me seemed taller, more athletic, as if they were chiselled from the very essence of fitness. The imposter syndrome had returned: how had I expected to compete with these guys and girls?

I later found out the exact statistics – out of more than 1,600 registered participants, only 1,272 had actually made it to the start line. By being here, I had progressed further than many had done, including my past self. However, a sobering reality loomed – that year like most others, about 15 per cent of Ironman participants didn't finish the race after starting it. As I looked around, it was a daunting realisation that, statistically, not all of us gathered here would see the finish line. In fact, for every ten people I saw in front of me, only eight or nine people would make it.

I remembered my coach's advice and did everything to push those thoughts aside; I focused on the task at hand. The pro athletes had already taken to the water, shooting off at speed around Pennington Flash. After around a 20-minute slow shuffle forward, it was finally our turn. The moment had arrived; it was time to start my Ironman journey.

As I discarded my face mask, a symbolic gesture of leaving behind the world of restrictions and uncertainties, I stepped forward towards the water. The nerves, the anticipation, the months of training – it all converged into this singular moment. I was about to embark on the most physically challenging day of my life – a real test of endurance, willpower and spirit. I took a deep breath, the sounds of the crowds around me. The Ironman UK had officially begun for me, and there was no turning back.

Chapter 39
The Swim – A Dance in the Deep

With my mask now a distant memory and my goggles and swim cap securely in place, I approached the water's edge of Pennington Flash. The Ironman swim starts in a rather unceremonious fashion – a walk over the timing mat, a quick slide down a plastic ramp, and a plunge into the water. It's less a heroic dive and more a pragmatic entry into the day's first challenge.

Any semblance of a plan to remain calm was immediately washed away by the cold shock of the water and the chaos of the swim start. It's one thing to train in open water, quite another to be in the thick of an Ironman swim surrounded by hundreds of competitors. As I took a moment to glance up after a few minutes, all I could see were banks of people in the water stretched out in front of me. Against all of my better judgement, I allowed myself a glance back and already there was a wave of people chasing me as we swam away from the starting pontoon. The lack of races due to Covid-19 meant that for many of us this was our first mass start in a long time. Additionally, in the few triathlons I had done up to this moment, all the swims had started with us bobbing in the water, acclimatised to the cold. Suddenly, I was amidst a flurry of arms and legs, an aquatic mosh pit where personal space was a forgotten luxury, in very cold waters just moments after being in relative warmth on land.

As per the wise words of Coach Garrie, I veered to the right by a few metres, seeking a sliver of open water where I could calm myself and find my rhythm amidst the splashes and jostles. Breathing became a conscious effort, each inhale a calculated move to avoid a mouthful of water. As the minutes ticked by, I finally started to feel my heart-rate settle. It was now or never I thought. I really didn't want my

Ironman journey to end with the moment getting to me and making me forget everything I had learned, resulting in me being pulled out of the water or failing to make the cut-off.

As I approached the buoy I had pointed out to Craig earlier, I realised my grave miscalculation – it was merely a marker in the water, not the turn I had anticipated. The actual turning point was still a significant distance away. Slightly deflated but undeterred, I pushed on, my strokes trying to find a steady tempo.

Rounding the first turn, I sneaked a glance at my watch. The time was slower than I had hoped, the chaotic start and flustered breathing having taken their toll. But now, in slightly more open water, I hoped to make up some time. The rhythm of my stroke became my focus, each pull through the water a step closer to the end of this 2.4-mile journey.

As I left the first buoy behind and set my sights on the next, the swim began to feel less like a battle and more like the familiar rhythm of training sessions. This stretch was shorter, the turn buoy ahead acting as a beacon in the murky waters. Sighting in this part of the swim became easier, and I found a semblance of peace amidst the flurry of arms and legs.

Around the second turn, I knew I had just one straight line swim to make it back to the shore, ahead of lap two. However, as I closed in on the final stretch of water a new challenge emerged. I felt something odd and unsettling around my legs – a sensation of something flapping against me. I knew that despite the wildlife that existed in the lake, this was unlikely to be the Loch Ness Monster of Pennington and was something else. Panic surged through me as my mind raced to the worst-case scenario: my timing chip must be coming loose. We had been told to wear this timing chip on our ankles, velcro'd tight. However, to make sure it tracked successfully, were under strict instructions to wear it on the outside of the wetsuit. The thought of emerging from the water, chip-less, and facing potential disqualification haunted me. Despite me swatting up on the rules as if I was to face an exam in all things Ironman, I had no idea what would happen if I emerged without a timing chip. Would I be allowed to continue without an official record of my swim time? Could this technical mishap undo all my efforts? Or best case, would I be allowed to continue but lose precious minutes as I waited for another timing chip to be set up and fetched over to me?

In a moment of panic and desperation, I flipped on to my back, fumbling with the Velcro strap around my ankle. It seemed fine, unmoved from where I had positioned it. I was immediately relieved that I wasn't facing the unknown or returning to land without it. My heart raced as I tightened it, flipped back around again, and tried to regain the rhythm and momentum I had lost. Barely a few minutes later, it repeated. Again, I stopped, trying to pull away from the oncoming swimmers to avoid being flattened and checked my chip again. As before, despite what I had felt, the chip and its strap seemed to have remained in place, what on earth was going on? Was I experiencing some bizarre Ironman paranoia right in the middle of the swim?

It was moments later that I realised it hadn't been loose at all. I had been swimming through a patch of aquatic plants, their tendrils brushing against my legs in the water. I mentally kicked myself for the lost time over a false alarm, two pauses in the water and losing my momentum. However, there was no time left to dwell on it. I resumed my mission to complete the lap, trying to push the incident to the back of my mind.

Only in an Ironman could you find yourself wrestling with lake weeds and paranoia in equal measure. But such are the trials of open-water swimming – it's not just about physical endurance, but also about handling the unexpected, whether it be a crowd of swimmers or a rogue patch of lake foliage. The initial panic and the weed debacle had cost me some time, but the race was far from over. I concentrated on my strokes, each pull through the water bringing me closer to the end of the swim leg.

As the pontoon came into view, marking the end of my first lap, I felt a surge of energy. Knowing that I was approaching halfway through the swim section of the Ironman UK, I picked up the pace, eager to finish that first lap as best I could.

Ironman UK, like many other long-course triathlons, features an 'Aussie exit' for two-lap swim courses. This unique element involves swimming to the edge of the water at the end of the first lap, exiting the water briefly on to a pontoon, and then jumping/sliding back in for the second lap. It's a relatively quick transition and it allows athletes a momentary respite from the surrounding water, an opportunity to recalibrate and refocus before plunging back into the swim.

As I approached the ramp for the Aussie exit, a volunteer's hand reached out to me, a much-welcomed human connection amidst the solitude of the swim and the unwelcomed crashes I had largely avoided but which had surrounded me menacingly so far. Their grip was firm and reassuring as they helped me out of the water. I jogged over the timing mat and a reassuring beep from the mat as I went told me that clearly the chip was still there, and alive and kicking. After such a long time surrounded by the quiet of the lake, head submerged in the water, the roar of the crowd and music was intense. Taking this brief moment on land to assess my progress, I allowed myself a quick glance at my watch – just under 45 minutes. It was an acceptable time, on track for my plan B, but not as fast as I had hoped given my ambitious aims after the last few weeks of progress. The swim had presented more challenges than anticipated, and it had showed in my time.

However, I could afford very little time to dwell on what could have been. I was under the cut-off time so far but I had lap two to begin and that would take me to my biggest open-water distance covered. I also needed to bank as much time as possible ahead of my next challenge. I readied myself for the second lap, determined to make up for lost time. With a deep breath, I slid back into the cold waters of Pennington Flash.

The second lap was a chance to reset, to apply the lessons learned from the first. I focused on maintaining a steady rhythm, avoiding the fray and navigating more efficiently. I had overcome the weeds, the crowds and my own doubts. Now, it was time to finish the job and ideally claw back some precious minutes.

Chapter 40
The Second Swim Lap -
Triumphs and Tribulations

Jumping back into the water of Pennington Flash for the second lap of the Ironman UK swim, I was greeted by a much calmer field. The frenzied start of the race had given way to a more settled rhythm and by this point the fastest pro swimmers had exited the water while the fastest amateur swimmers were already well through their second lap allowing for more space. Now acclimatised to the cold water of the Flash and buoyed by the adrenaline of the first lap, I felt more confident, more in control. The first couple of buoys were navigated with relative ease, the path ahead clearer and less congested than before.

As I turned at the third buoy and headed for the final stretch of the swim, the distant sounds of music from the starting line reached my ears. Of all the sounds to be hit with, it was 'Timber', Kesha and Pitbull's energetic song, that became an unexpected soundtrack to the final leg of my swim, every other stroke as I lifted my head out of the water to breathe. Oddly, the music stirred a wave of emotion in me. Here I was, nearing the completion of the swim leg, something that had once seemed like an insurmountable challenge, and I was being serenaded by Pitbull. I want to point out it was more the realisation of how close I was to the end of the Ironman swim that stirred that emotion! Until this moment I hadn't really been that bothered about Pitbull and Kesha's catchy number, but from that moment on I bloody loved it!

But just as I was riding this wave of triumph, an unforeseen obstacle emerged – a rogue swimmer. I'd made it 80 per cent through the Ironman swim, avoiding the rumoured physical battle with the other swimmers, but on the last stretch, this fella had other ideas and managed to disrupt my rhythm while I was in the midst of sighting the pontoon. First of all, I noticed him out of my peripheral vision, swimming oddly close to where I was. Despite the rest of us all swimming in straight and direct lines, shooting towards the pontoon, he was seemingly off-course and veered undeterred directly towards me. The impact was sudden – a harsh blow to the side of my head, as he chopped through the water, either unknowing or with a lack of care. He ploughed on and, for a brief moment, the red mist clouded my vision.

I was tempted to retaliate, to let out the frustration over this unexpected collision in some way. God knows how I planned to do this, we were still a couple of hundred metres from shore and we all looked exactly the same. I am generally seen as a very nice guy, but when anger hits, I am known to hold my own (some people call it short-man syndrome!). But a moment of clarity washed over me – I was less than two hours into what would likely be a very long, gruelling day for me. It was no time for wasted energy, both physically and mentally, or for short-sighted reactions. Any immediate satisfaction would be far outweighed by the long-term cost to my race. I paused, caught my breath, shook away the blow to the head and refocused on the task at hand.

Pushing through the final metres, I swam towards the pontoon with renewed determination. The end of the swim leg was in sight and I was not going to let anything, not even a wayward swimmer, derail me now. As I reached the exit, hands reached out to pull me from the water once more, a welcome assist as I transitioned back to solid ground after a fair amount of time being horizontal in the water.

Crossing over the timing mat, I clocked an official time of 1:28:46. It wasn't the ambitious sub-1:20 I had dreamed of, but it was a time I could be proud of. My calls with Coach Garrie on race strategy were valuable for this reason.

We had agreed anything under 1 hour 30 minutes was a victory in my book, especially considering the challenges the swim had presented.

The swim leg, my Achilles heel in the triathlon world, was behind me. I had faced cold waters, crowded fields and even a swimmer gone rogue, yet here I was, ready to tackle the next part of the Ironman challenge. But there was no time to waste, I ripped off the goggles and the swim cap and away I went, jogging towards transition, getting used to being on land and trying to keep up my positive start to the day.

Entering the first transition (T1) after my swim, I would have sworn I had learned my lessons of triathlons past, my days of flapping around trying to get out of wetsuits long behind me. What I didn't realise was that my T1 would turn out to be a significant chunk of time – officially over 14 minutes! If on departing I'd have been asked how long I'd spent in transition I'd have estimated a quick five minutes or so, the average being eight minutes. But somewhere between the wetsuit peel-off and the transition tent, time had slipped away, nibbling into my buffer without my knowledge. Thankfully I was blissfully unaware of my laboured attempts at this, still beaming from the confidence of coming in 50 minutes under the swim cut-off. I had banked that towards the cycle I thought, not knowing I had lost five minutes to my post-swim dillydallying!

I certainly hadn't given the same level of attention to transitions as swimming, biking and running. However, there were a few mitigating factors that may excuse at least some of those minutes. In the transition tent, I opted for a complete change. Unlike many triathletes who wear their tri suits under their wetsuits for a speedy turnover, I followed Coach Garrie's advice. I exchanged my wetsuit for specific, and more importantly, dry cycling gear. This included slightly more padded shorts, aiming for comfort during the long ride ahead, while crucially not being wet would reduce the risk of any chafing.

And then, perhaps the real time sink: I sat down to devour a bagel smothered in jam and peanut butter. In my mind, replenishing those 900 or so calories I'd burned in the swim was crucial. If nothing else, after an hour and a half of only being exposed to the culinary delights of the Pennington Flash water, it tasted bloody amazing! It was a calculated decision: a few extra minutes for a more comfortable and energised bike leg seemed like a good trade-off.

The weather had remained dry so far, but I wasn't taking any chances. I knew at some point at least this was likely to change. I stashed a small fold-up rain jacket in the back pocket of my cycling jersey, just in case the skies decided to open up. Helmet and sunglasses on, I checked over my bike one last time before wheeling it towards the exit. It was almost time to mount up and tackle the 112-mile ride.

However, Ironman then offered a stark reminder of its relentless unpredictability. As I was about to exit T1, the event compere's voice broke through the buzz of the transition area, making a plea for anyone who had a spare wheel or bike. An unusual request, I later got the full story from Briony. A fellow athlete, fresh from her swim success, had grabbed her bike, only to find at some point several spokes had dislodged, making her bike unrideable. It was a heart-wrenching story, for someone to have come so far, underscoring the cruelty that can sometimes accompany the sport. I hope she found a solution and was able to continue her race.

For me, I made my way to the mount line, I heard the shouts from my little support crew on the sidelines and gave them a quick wave so they would know I was feeling okay after the swim. It was time to leave T1 behind and begin the next chapter of this Ironman story. The bike leg awaited, a journey of 112 miles through the Lancashire countryside, a test of endurance, strategy and sheer will.

As I clicked in and started pedalling, it was quite an emotional feeling knowing after all those hours the swim part of my journey had now been completed. From the chilly waters of Pennington Flash to the bustling T1, every step was a learning experience, a testament to the journey of Ironman. Now, with the road stretching out before me, I was ready to embrace the challenge, to pedal through every mile with the same determination that had brought me this far.

The Ironman UK continued, and I was in it, fully committed to every turn of the pedal, every hill and every moment of this incredible adventure.

Chapter 41
The Bike Leg - A Journey of Hills, Cheers and Cobbles

Mounting my bike for the 112-mile cycling leg of Ironman UK, I started with the stretch from Pennington Flash to Bolton. This section served as a gentle introduction to what lay ahead, with a few undulating hills but nothing too severe. It was a pleasant surprise to find streets lined with friendly faces, their cheers and well-wishes injecting an extra dose of energy into my pedalling. This early part of the course provided the perfect opportunity to get acclimatised to the bike, begin my nutrition strategy and build up some momentum before tackling the more challenging laps ahead. Nutrition wise, I focused on one bottle of clear water and one full of a carb and electrolyte mix. The plan was to cycle through a bottle every 45 mins, rotating through the combination.

The weather, much to my relief, remained dry. The conditions were ideal for cycling and I took advantage of this as I dropped on to Chorley New Road. This stretch, familiar from my virtual training sessions on Rouvy, offering what I knew was the only fast and flat reprieve in a course known for its relentless hills. I felt a sense of déjà vu as I cycled this familiar road, a testament to the hours spent in my makeshift home training set-up.

Entering Bolton town centre, I ventured into a segment of the course I had only experienced in the virtual world. During my practice rides, the groups I was with had deliberately avoided this busy area, knowing that navigating it pre-Ironman, with its constant traffic lights and general hustle and bustle of any large town, would take up way too much time, when really it was only a short stretch of a mile or so. The town centre offered a fantastic opportunity for spectators to see the cyclists up close but, as I pedalled through, the reality of the cobbled streets hit me – quite literally. Every bone in my body rattled as I navigated the uneven surface, my bottle cage clanging in protest. 'Who thought cobbles were a good idea for a bike course?' I muttered under my breath, trying to maintain balance and momentum.

Soon I got over myself, and despite the jarring cobbles there was something special about cycling through the heart of Bolton with the energy of the crowds, the sound of clapping and cheering, providing a much-needed morale boost.

Leaving the cobbled streets of Bolton town centre behind, I was immediately greeted by an unexpected and slightly surreal sight – an aid station. That in itself, on an Ironman, should not be unexpected they are placed throughout the course offering freshly filled water bottles, energy gels and such like. But this one was manned by a gaggle of Oompa Loompas! Yes, you read that right. At least 30 of them. There they were, in all their orange-skinned, green-haired glory, offering water and nutrition with wide, chocolate-factory grins. It was one of those bizarre Ironman moments when you question if you're in a race or a Roald Dahl novel. Had I made it out of the swim, or was this a crazy hallucination while I sat in a hospital bed! I grabbed a water bottle from an outstretched orange Oompa Loompa hand, half expecting it to taste like fizzy lifting drinks.

Once past the Willy Wonka-inspired aid station, it was time to face the first serious test of the bike leg – the long climb towards Bolton Golf Course and into the heart of the Lancashire hills. This stretch of road was familiar territory for me, thanks to my countless virtual and real-world training sessions. Each blind turn on the ascent was etched in my memory, a series of mental markers that guided me up the hill. Knowing the length of the climb was a small comfort, as each turn hid the peak, making the ascent seem endless.

As I approached the last daunting ascent, I mentally braced myself for a tough final push. However, to my surprise and delight, the road was lined with a tunnel of supporters from the Rochdale Tri club. Their presence was like a sudden jolt of energy. Cowbells rang, music blared as the crowd's enthusiastic cheers and shouts created an electrifying atmosphere that seemed to physically pull me up the hill, which they flanked on both sides, creating a narrow chute for us to file through. I found myself responding to their energy, fist-pumping and shouting back, carried forward by the wave of support.

This unexpected boost from the local triathlon club was more than just a pleasant surprise. It was a powerful reminder of the camaraderie and community spirit that makes Ironman races so special. For a moment, the gruelling climb felt effortless, my bike propelled forward by the collective enthusiasm of the supporters.

I crested the hill, still riding the high of the crowd's energy; I couldn't help but smile at the absurdity and beauty of it all. There I was in the middle of a gruelling Ironman race, having just been cheered on by Oompa Loompas and a throng of passionate triathlon fans that made me feel like a Tour de France champion. It was these moments, these unexpected bursts of joy and human connection, that made the long hours of training and the pain of the race all worthwhile.

With the first major climb conquered and the cheers of the tri club still echoing in my ears, I pressed on. The hills of Lancashire continued to roll out before me, each one a new challenge to face. But now, buoyed by the support and the surreal experiences of the race so far, I felt ready to tackle whatever came next. The bike leg of Ironman UK was unfolding into an adventure filled with surprises, and I was all-in for the ride.

Now the course transitioned into a quieter, more introspective stretch. This part of the route required a shift in focus. The roads were closed to any cars or lorries that day so it felt eerily silent, devoid of the earlier cheers and music. It was a stark contrast to the bustling town centre and the lively support from the Oompa Loompas and enthusiastic fans.

Here, the race became a solitary journey. The other athletes, while present, were spaced out at the regulation distances imposed to stop drafting and any rider gaining an unfair advantage. Each rider seemed lost in their own world of endurance and determination. The lack of external distractions meant that my thoughts and the rhythmic sound of my pedalling were my only companions.

The road meandered through occasional small towns, which provided brief respites from the monotony as locals came out to clap and cheer. However, the vast majority of this section was long stretches of road and the absence of crowds meant that there were no cheers to carry me forward, no music to lift my spirits. Just the open road and me, accompanied by the occasional whoosh of another cyclist passing by or the soft buzz of a drone capturing the event from above.

Bolton's landscape doesn't lend itself to flat, easy rides. It's a terrain defined by its relentless undulations – a series of small descents followed by sharp turns and an unending succession of uphill challenges. Each climb tested my resolve, and each descent offered a fleeting moment of respite before the next ascent began. The course was a true test of mental and physical stamina, a continuous cycle of exertion and brief recovery.

Approaching the final significant incline of the lap, Sheephouse Lane loomed ahead, infamous for its challenging ascent and rapid descent. The beginning of the climb was marked by a sharp turn on to a steep hill by a pub called the Black Dog. Much like a scene from the Tour de France, supporters were thronged along the roadside creating a claustrophobic tunnel leading upwards. Their presence was a welcome sight, their cheers a much-needed boost as I began the arduous climb with their sounds booming around me.

Amongst the crowd, I spotted Coach Garrie and his crew. They were strategically positioned to offer encouragement at this critical point in the race. Their familiar faces and enthusiastic cheers energised me as I tackled one of the most notorious sections of the Ironman UK course.

Sheephouse Lane, revered for its challenging gradient, was a steady rise to the top of the third and final big hill of my first lap. The hills looked breathtaking, as I reached the peak, but at the summit of this famous ascent I encountered a different type of sight, one that was certainly not from any guide book. It was one of the unique spectacles that Ironman UK promises – the Mexican wrestlers.

This peculiar tradition has become a hallmark of Bolton's Ironman, where a group of enthusiastic locals, dressed as flamboyant *luchadores*, cheer on the athletes. Known as the Sheephouse Lane Fancy Dress Party, they are a colourful crew that gets into position overnight, sets up their camper van and music and waits to give the athletes support. Their colourful masks and vibrant costumes stood in stark contrast to the grey skies, bringing a slice of Mexican fiesta to the Lancashire countryside. They have become such a famous part of Ironman UK, the medal even bore their (masked) faces one year. The music blared as these masked-up, topless men danced, grooved and waved signs declaring 'you're my favourite'. Their presence was both absurd and uplifting, a bizarre yet delightful diversion from the physical strain of the climb.

After the surreal encounter with the Mexican wrestlers, the course led to a rapid descent back towards the town. This was a section where nerves of steel were required. Again, in my virtual practice sessions where crashing was impossible, I could make up time and leave the brakes untouched. However, in the real world, the road, notorious for its potholes and cattle grids, made for a particularly hazardous descent. I gripped my handlebars tightly, focused on navigating the treacherous terrain safely while maintaining a good pace, topping over 30mph as the landscape blurred behind me.

As I descended the final miles of the lap, I reflected on how well the first lap had gone. Genuinely I was pretty happy. First and foremost, my Boardman bike had become trusted once more. Gear changes were a breeze, and so far there had been no issues with the tyres. As for my nutrition, I had stayed on track. My energy levels felt fine and, despite the challenging hills, I had largely been in Coach Garrie's recommended heart zones. But just as I was settling into a rhythm, the weather decided to throw a curveball. The first few rain drops were a gentle warning of what was to come. Within minutes, the drizzle turned into a downpour, the rain coming down in biblical proportions.

Now, as I descended back towards Bolton the rain was relentless, drenching me to the bone. Visibility decreased, and the roads, already challenging, became slick and even more treacherous. The change in weather added a new layer of complexity to the race and I realised that, despite my perceived success on the first lap, laps two and three were to be a completely different kettle of fish. What had started as a challenging but manageable ride was now a battle against the elements.

Despite the worsening conditions, I pressed on, determined not to let the rain dampen my spirits even if it had soaked my clothing. I had not come this far for a little (a lot of) rain to spoil my party. The mental image of the Mexican wrestlers cheering on the sidelines served as a reminder of the joyful absurdity and unexpected moments that make Ironman races so memorable and I wanted more.

The Ironman was proving to be every bit the challenge I had anticipated, but I was meeting it head-on, one raindrop and one mile at a time. I braced myself for what lay ahead, ready to face the rain, the hills and whatever else the course had in store. Lap one was complete, bring on lap two!

Chapter 42
The Soaking Second Lap

As I commenced the second lap of the Ironman UK bike course, the rain truly transformed from being a nuisance into an adversary. While it's common in stories like this to embellish conditions and create a narrative to amplify achievements into something more significant, I assure you no exaggeration was needed here! It seemed as if the heavens had opened up just to challenge the Ironman athletes. Probably not so surprisingly, if you seek out any of the promotional videos for Ironman UK, you'll often see the sunshine and smiles, but any footage of this downpour in Bolton is conspicuously absent. Clearly, a rain-soaked day in Bolton doesn't make for the most enticing marketing material!

I knew it was bad when I pedalled up the hills and a stream of water cascaded down towards me as the drains overflowed with the sheer volume, turning the roads into part-rivers. It was a scenario I had never trained in because, quite frankly, who would willingly cycle in such conditions? If you were to look outside your bedroom window and see this, you'd quite simply head to the turbo trainer or back to bed. It wouldn't be safe or sensible to be out in it. This part of the race became one of the most daunting and intense experiences of my sporting life.

The first major challenge was navigating the cobbled streets of Bolton town centre. Now not just an annoying bouncy part of the course, they were slick with rain and demanded cautious and slow navigation. I felt like I was inching along at a snail's pace, each turn a calculated risk to avoid slipping. Riders clogged up as we balanced the need not to lose minutes but also a desire to stay upright.

Leaving the treacherous cobbles behind, I soon noticed a disconcerting rattle coming from my bike, I ignored it as best I could but as it grew louder and louder, eventually I admitted defeat and knew I needed to address it. Concerned after my recent bike mechanical issues, I pulled into the next aid station for a quick assessment. The first thing I did was ditch my budget-friendly Decathlon glasses; while the cheap lenses had resolved any issues with sun glare, they had quickly fogged up in the rain and were now completely redundant. I pulled out my rain jacket to protect me as well as possible from the worsening conditions and began to investigate the source of the rattle.

Upon inspection, I discovered that one of my bottle cages had become a casualty of the cobbled streets. It had loosened and was now dangling precariously, one solo bolt remaining, the others long gone. With no spare screws to fix it, I had no other choice. I removed the last remaining screw, and pulled off the cage, resigned to tossing my carbon holder and second bottle into a nearby bin. My nutrition plan was now reduced to a single-bottle strategy – not ideal, not what I was used to, but now necessary.

As I resumed my ride, the single-bottle nutrition plan weighed on my mind. I had meticulously planned my energy intake for the race, and this hiccup required a quick mental adjustment. I had to ration my remaining bottle and make the most of the aid stations. On the plus side, it was one less bottle to carry up the hills.

Despite these challenges, a strange sense of togetherness developed among the riders and volunteers at the aid stations. We were all battling the same torrential rain, the same slippery roads and facing our own unique setbacks. Shouts of encouragement and empathetic nods were exchanged as we passed each other, an acknowledgment of the shared struggle we found ourselves in.

Now for the part of the story I am sure you all have been waiting for. As I pedalled away on the Ironman bike course, I came to the point where nature called. Not the 'admire the scenic Lancashire countryside' kind of nature call, but the more pressing, bladder-screaming kind. So, I faced the dilemma many Ironmen and Ironwomen face: to pee or not to pee!

Now for your typical 'time-is-of-the-essence-every-second-counts' Ironman athlete, one does not simply stop for a leisurely bathroom break. However, I was not breaking any records today and, for the first time in my life, the idea of pulling up and entering the protection of a Portaloo seemed very appealing.

However, given that the heavens had opened up and it was pouring, the alternative was to pee while I rode along. I thought, 'Well, when else will I get a better chance to blend in?' The rain was coming down in sheets, turning the roads into miniature rivers and my bike into a makeshift submarine. In this aquatic adventure, a little extra liquid wouldn't be noticed, right? Plus, I knew the moment I got off the bike, the temptation to never, ever, EVER get back on would kick in.

So, there I was, cycling through the storm, deciding to embrace the full Ironman experience. It felt like trying to pat your head and rub your stomach simultaneously, but on wheels and at speed. I learned there's an art to it, a sort of Zen-like focus needed to relax while maintaining balance and speed (plus avoiding my remaining water bottle). As the warm sensation provided a brief respite from the cold rain, I couldn't help but chuckle at the absurdity of this day, this wet and wild experience that it had become.

The rain had another unintended consequence – it became the great equaliser. Everyone was drenched, whether from the sky or their own doing. Fellow cyclists whizzed by, expressions of intense concentration on their faces and I wondered how many were deep in race concentration or whether they were partaking in the same clandestine activity as me.

Post-pee, with a renewed sense of lightness, I powered on. The rain continued to hammer down, washing away any evidence of my mid-race escapade. It was a moment of Ironman ingenuity, a blend of necessity and opportunity, a story that would later bring bouts of laughter when shared with friends. Because, at the end of the day, what's an Ironman without a little rain, a little pee and a lot of determination?

The rain at this stage showed no signs of letting up. Here I was, soaked to the bone, tackling one of the most challenging athletic events out there, in the midst of a downpour that seemed almost comically timed. Each turn of the pedal was a small victory, each mile covered a step closer to the end of this drenched ordeal. The second lap of the bike course was turning out to be a test of endurance and adaptability, but I was determined to see it through, come rain or high water.

The downpour had drastically reduced visibility and the wet conditions made slowing and braking a precarious endeavour, especially on this technical course. I had to approach each section with extra caution, constantly adjusting to the evolving risks the weather imposed.

It was during one of these cautious stretches that I witnessed the first significant accident of the day. This part of the route, which I remembered vividly from my training loop ride earlier in the year (the scene of the fallen chain and red faces), featured a small downhill section leading into a sharp right turn. The key to navigating this part was to resist the temptation to build up speed on the descent, ensuring enough time to control the tight corner. Unfortunately, it seemed someone hadn't managed this delicate balance.

As I approached the area, the flashing lights of an ambulance and paramedics at work painted a grim picture. A shattered wooden fence, a crumpled bike and a huddle of first responders indicated a serious accident. It was a sobering sight and a stark reminder of the fine line we were all treading between pushing our limits and staying within the bounds of safety. The bike and its rider had by the looks of it become the victims of the worsening conditions on an already challenging course. It was clear that their race day was over.

As I cautiously pedalled past the scene, I reflected on the inherent risks of endurance cycling, especially under such adverse conditions. This incident brought home the reality that, despite our best preparations and the roads being closed to cars, the unpredictable nature of a race – compounded by inclement weather – could bring unexpected hazards.

Later, when I read race reviews and forum discussions, I learned that some athletes had anticipated the Ironman might be cancelled mid-race due to the rapidly deteriorating conditions. Perhaps it was my singular focus on completing the race, or maybe a touch of naivety about the potential dangers, but I had never considered the possibility of a cancellation once it had begun.

The severity of the weather and its impact on the riders was encapsulated by two stories I heard later that day, each illustrating the challenge posed by the conditions.

The first story revolved around a fellow athlete's encounter at an aid station. As the relentless rain continued to drench and chill the riders to the bone, one cyclist, visibly shivering and soaked through, pulled over to refill his water bottle. A paramedic, noticing the rider's condition, approached with concern. The cyclist's shivering was so severe that the paramedic asked him to demonstrate his ability to operate his brakes fully and safely. When the rider struggled to achieve this to a satisfactory standard, the paramedic made the tough call. If the rider couldn't operate his brakes properly, he wouldn't be allowed back on the course, for the safety of him and the fellow riders.

Wrapped in a foil blanket, the rider sat at the aid station, time ticking away as he tried desperately to warm up and regain control over his trembling body. The minutes stretched on, each one precious and irreplaceable in a race against the clock. Finally, after what he said felt like an eternity, the paramedics allowed him to retry, and deemed him fit to continue his race.

The second story came from another fellow participant, who candidly admitted to seeking refuge in a Portaloo during the ride. Two-thirds into the gruelling course, they retreated to the temporary shelter for a brief respite from the relentless onslaught of the rain. Inside the cramped confines of the Portaloo, away from the chaos of the race, they experienced their lowest moment. Overcome with exhaustion, frustration at the conditions and the sheer weight of the challenge, they broke down and cried.

These stories painted a vivid picture of the day's harsh realities. They spoke of the physical and emotional toll that the combination of an Ironman and adverse weather can exact. As I neared the end of the second lap, the impact of the rain was evident in my pace. I was travelling significantly slower than I had hoped. But it wasn't just about slower times; the conditions had transformed the course into a veritable obstacle course of cycling challenges.

Every turn of the road seemed to reveal a new scene of struggle. Cyclists were dotted along the route, their bikes upturned as they hurriedly worked to replace punctured inner tubes. The notorious roads of Bolton, known for their unforgiving potholes, had become even more treacherous in the wet conditions. The race organisers had made efforts to fill the worst of the potholes and had marked the remaining untreated holes with bright blue spray paint so we could spot them in advance and avoid. However, the continuous downpour had washed away these warnings, leaving riders to navigate the perilous terrain blind.

The descents, challenging enough on a dry day, had become particularly scary. What had been nerve-wracking but manageable on the first lap was now a gauntlet of unexpected dangers. Scattered along the downhill stretches were water bottles that had fallen from other cyclists' bikes. These unexpected obstacles added an extra layer of risk to each descent. Every downward slope became a tense exercise in caution, as I tried to avoid both the potholes and the bike debris that littered the road.

Despite the challenges, I pressed on, driven by the singular focus of completing this lap and moving one step closer to the final stretch of the bike course. In Ironman circles this course has a reputation for being one of the tougher ones, with its hills and technical descents. Throw in the adverse weather conditions and it was living up to its reputation, and then some. As I pedalled through the rain, I found a new level of respect for my fellow athletes and the journey we were all undertaking. In the face of adversity, we were all pushing our limits, united by a common goal and the shared experience of this gruelling race.

Entering the third and final lap of the Ironman UK bike course, I was greeted with a slight reprieve from the weather. The rain, though still present, had eased up a bit. I was still thoroughly soaked from head to toe and, after nearly six hours of relentless pedalling, I decided to take my first real stop of the race.

I unclipped from my pedals and carefully parked my bike at one of the designated areas. It was time to access my special needs bag – a small trove of essentials I had packed as answers to all the 'what if' scenarios that could unfold during the race. Bypassing the plasters and spare inner tubes, which thankfully remained unnecessary, I reached for the real treasure I had stashed away: a huge chicken, hummus and gherkin baguette. Though it was a day old, the combination of salt, protein and carbs was exactly what my body craved. Taking a bite, it was, without exaggeration, one of the best things I had ever tasted. If you ever want to have the best sandwich of your life, all you need to do is cycle 80-odd miles in torrential rain, powered by tasteless gels and sickly-sweet energy drinks to really unleash those taste buds!

I silently thanked Coach Garrie in that moment. His insider knowledge and advice on the importance of real food during such a gruelling event was invaluable. It was another huge advantage gained from the incredible weekend training event he had put on. The simple sandwich was a stark contrast to the carb mixes, gels and bananas that had been my only source of nutrition since my T1 bagel. This baguette was a much-needed physical and mental boost at this point in the day, especially considering the 3,500 calories I had already burned.

Feeling slightly rejuvenated, I prepared to embark on the last lap. I repacked my special needs bag, discarding the remnants of my sandwich and securing everything else back in place, shoving a few extra gels into my pockets. I took a moment to stretch my legs, giving them a brief respite from the constant cycling motion. The brief pause also gave me a chance to mentally prepare for the final stretch. I knew this lap would be crucial; it was the last big push before transitioning to the marathon. I was on track to beat the cut-off but one slip-up could still cost me.

As I started that final lap of the course, I soon realised that my ideal pace time achieved in lap one was out of reach and it was going to be a slow journey to the finish. The weather had eased, but the toll of the previous hours had set in, not just for me but for many of my fellow competitors. The fatigue was visible on the faces and in the movements of the riders around me.

One particular instance stood out starkly as we approached the first major hill. I saw a fellow athlete struggling halfway up. He had unclipped from his pedals and was catching his breath. As I neared him, he attempted to clip back in and resume his ride. However, he only managed a few more metres before losing momentum and tumbling on to the grass verge beside the road. Concerned, I tried to keep going (I knew if I stopped on this hill, I had little chance of getting going again myself) but called out to him, asking if he was alright. He responded with a weary but jaded thumbs-up. I turned back as he sat dejectedly next to his bike. It was a relief to see that he was physically alright but I knew the day had taken a toll on him, and with most of the final lap still to go, it was going to be a difficult challenge to get to the finish line.

At this stage of the race, the strict pacing strategy that I had adhered to for so long had become secondary. My primary focus had shifted to simply keeping my head down and pushing forward, one pedal stroke at a time. The goal was no longer about maintaining a specific pace, it was about making it to the cut-off point before time ran out. Every turn of the pedal, every incline and every descent brought me closer to the end of this gruelling bike segment.

As I approached the 100-mile mark, my energy was waning and my spirits were flagging. It had been seven hours of barely any communication beyond the passing greetings. With no music allowed and most of the crowds reduced in size due to the weather, it was just myself, my bike and my thoughts. It had been a cold and lonely place and I was beginning to feel it. That's when, to my surprise and delight, I spotted a familiar face among the sparse roadside crowd. My boss, Alan Harding, was there, with his three boys in tow, braving the light rain to cheer me on. Their presence was unexpected and incredibly heartening. He had not mentioned coming out to support, and to think that they had made the journey, stood in the unpleasant weather, just for a brief glimpse of me as I cycled past, was incredibly touching.

Their cheers and waves gave me a much-needed boost. Suddenly, the last ten miles didn't seem as daunting. I felt a renewed sense of determination and gratitude. Alan's gesture reminded me of the incredible support circle I had during my training and the people rooting for me during this race. It was moments like these that truly underscored the generosity of certain people in your life, when it's most needed.

With this new-found energy, I powered through the final stretch of the bike course. Although the dreadful weather and the constant climbing had taken their toll on my time, I knew that at this point, as long as I could avoid any technical issues with the bike, somehow I was on track to make the cut-off. I shot down Chorley Lane, towards Transition Two outside Queens Park. Crossing the finish line of the bike segment, I checked my time: 7:58:44. While it wasn't the best time I had hoped for, it was once again just within the acceptable range I had discussed with Coach Garrie. Anything under eight hours was my goal, and I had managed to achieve it in race-day conditions worse than I could have possibly imagined.

I hadn't been able to bank any additional time during the bike leg, but that was secondary now. The important thing was that I had made the cut-off, and with a margin of 45 minutes to spare. Reflecting on the race later on in the week, I learned that the bike segment had seen a notably high failure rate. Nearly 13 per cent of the field had missed the cut-off – the highest DNF rate at this point in the race in 12 years. The statistic was sobering, but it also underscored the challenge and unpredictability of this particular year's race.

As I transitioned from the bike to the run, I knew I had conquered one of the most challenging segments of the Ironman. The journey was far from over, but with the bike leg behind me, I felt ready to tackle the final challenge: the Ironman marathon.

Chapter 43

The T2 and Embarking on the Marathon

During the following week, as I looked back at the footage of my entrance into Transition 2 (T2) kindly recorded and sent to me by Ironman, I couldn't help but chuckle. There I was, heaving a sigh of relief so loud it was captured on the audio, marking the end of a gruelling bike leg.

I rolled my trusty Boardman bike to its designated spot, athlete 1168, and began the awkward waddle towards the transition tent to grab my T2 bag. Emerging from the tent, I was armed with more substantial snacks to break the monotony of gels and carb drinks that had been my sustenance for the past several hours.

As we now know from my exploits in Transition 1, throw me into a transition area and I somehow morph into a human sloth. This was once again proven by my recorded transition time. I still can't fathom how I managed to spend a whopping 16 minutes in T2! It's a mystery for the ages.

Then came the slightly bizarre ritual I had been advised to perform at the training weekend – spraying myself with deodorant after changing into my running gear. The theory was that smelling a bit fresher might trick my mind into feeling rejuvenated as I prepared for the marathon. At this point in the race, I was willing to try anything to breathe life into my body. However, as soon as the hiss of my deodorant can was released, it was met with audible chuckles and a few bemused glances from my fellow competitors. There I was, thinking a spritz of deodorant would somehow counteract ten hours of gruelling physical exertion – swimming in Pennington Flash and biking through the hills and rains of Bolton!

Exiting the transition, I couldn't help but chuckle at the absurdity of my deodorant application. But hey, every little psychological advantage counts, right? I glanced at my fellow competitors as I made my way out. Some looked as fresh as if they'd just started, while others bore the tell-tale signs of exhaustion. The reality of an Ironman had really begun to take its toll it seems. I turned to leave the tent, my hand tightly gripping a selection of gels – my energy lifeline for the run. Regardless of appearances, we were all united in the same daunting task ahead: the marathon.

As I started the run, it became apparent that my legs weren't entirely on board with this next phase of the Ironman just yet. They felt like two lead weights, more inclined to a leisurely stroll than a marathon run. The first few steps were a mix of jogging and a peculiar shuffle. I remembered Coach Garrie's advice: start slow, find your rhythm and don't be a hero at the start. So, I took it easy, allowing my body to adjust to this new form of torture.

The early part of the run took us through some of Bolton's streets, which, compared to the solitude of the bike course, felt like running through a carnival. Spectators lined the route, their cheers and claps providing a much-needed morale boost. One enthusiastic spectator, armed with a megaphone, was doling out a mix of encouragement and light-hearted banter. 'Come on, you've only got a marathon to go!' he bellowed, causing a few weary smiles among us runners.

As I settled into a somewhat steady pace, my Garmin watch beeped, indicating the completion of the first mile. There was a long old way to go, but it was the first of hopefully many small victories along the way. The first lap of the marathon was about finding my footing, understanding my body's limits and mentally preparing for the miles ahead. I reminded myself that this was what all the training, all the early mornings and late evenings, had been leading up to.

Entering Bolton town centre for the first time during the marathon leg of the Ironman felt like stepping on to a different planet. This was where dreams were being realised – the finish line of the Ironman UK.

The area was buzzing with energy. Supporters lined the streets, their cheers and applause creating a wall of sound that lifted the spirits of every weary athlete. I could see the fastest competitors, those superhumans, already crossing the finish line, while I had 25 miles to go. The iconic phrase 'You are an Ironman', announced by the compere in his booming voice, echoed through the air. Each time this famous saying was announced, a cheer and whoops erupted from the crowd. That was the moment I had dreamed of.

As I paced slowly but surely through the town centre and the scenes of the finishing area unfurled in front of me, the reality of my situation dawned on me. This was where I would, hopefully, end my journey later in the day. The thought alone sent a shiver of excitement mixed with apprehension down my spine.

Approaching the first of the aid stations, I made a tactical decision to walk. This wasn't going to be a personal-best marathon by any stretch of the imagination. The relentless Ironman course had already taken its toll on my body and, right now, no matter what it took, it was about getting to that finishing line.

As I walked through the aid station, I took the opportunity to grab some water and some energy gels to replenish my stock. I was determined to stick to my defined nutrition plan and avoid any gut problems that might be caused by trying something new on race day. It was a smorgasbord of running sugar and hydration and I certainly needed all the energy I could get. Around me, other athletes were doing the same, each lost in their own world of fatigue and determination.

I set off again, jogging at a conservative pace. I had to manage my energy carefully to make it through the marathon. My strategy was simple: jog the flats and downhills, walk the uphills and aid stations. It wasn't glamorous, but it was effective.

Entering Queens Park for the first time was a moment I had eagerly anticipated after a day largely in solitude. This was where I expected to see Craig, Briony and bump. The park, with its jubilant supporters and scenic backdrop, promised a brief respite from the gruelling marathon. It was also the ideal strategic spot for my supporters, since the course looped through the park twice per lap, meaning I would hopefully get eight opportunities to see them and receive a much-needed pick-me-up. However, as I ventured further along the marathon route, to my initial concern they were nowhere to be seen. In the normal run of things, Briony and I would be in constant contact through the day, but today, since plunging into the water in the early morning, there had been a complete communication blackout. I tried to push away any dark thoughts of pregnancy complications or anything else that had held them back.

Focusing back on the race, I took Coach Garrie's advice and walked up the steep incline that led through the final stretch of the park. Reaching the top, I emerged on to Chorley Road for the out-and-back section. Here, I found a steady rhythm, jogging consistently between aid stations, allowing myself brief moments of recovery before pushing on.

As I approached the end of the first lap, I was handed a green wristband – a simple yet significant token that marked the completion of lap one. In the Ironman, each lap earned you a different-coloured band, a visual indicator to marshals (and fellow participants) of your progress. This system kept track of the gruelling journey, lap by lap. It may seem to some a pointless addition, but trust me, after the day so far, it was quite easy to forget what lap you were on! No one would want to race down that finishers' chute only to be told to turn back around and complete another loop.

Re-entering Queens Park, the long-awaited moment finally arrived – I spotted Briony and Craig. Their shouts and cheers cut through the fatigue and brought a smile to my face. It was a moment of relief and joy, a much-needed emotional boost, meaning I was no longer concerned for their safety. Though I was tempted to stop for a chat, I was on a downhill stretch, and I didn't want to waste the opportunity to gain some speed with less effort! So, with a wave and a grateful nod, I pushed on, ready to tackle lap two.

As I left them behind, I felt a renewed sense of determination brought on by the briefest of interactions. The support of loved ones and the energy of the crowd were powerful motivators, urging me to keep moving, to keep pushing towards that finish line. With one lap down and three to go, I was one step closer to earning the title of Ironman. The journey was far from over, but with each stride, each cheer from the crowd and each coloured wristband, I was writing my own Ironman story – one filled with grit, resilience and a touch of humour amidst the exhaustion.

Chapter 44
Enduring the Middle Miles

The second lap of the marathon marked a shift in my Ironman journey. My pace had settled into a steady ten-minute mile, a significant drop from my earlier enthusiasm of lap one and the first seven-odd miles, but comfortably ahead of what was required to avoid the dreaded cut-off time of 17 hours. The relentless downpour that had plagued the bike leg had now eased into a lighter drizzle, a small mercy from the weather gods. However, this respite came with its own challenge: the cool air that accompanied the rain had intensified, making my damp clothes cling to me with an uncomfortable chill, which provided me with added motivation to keep moving.

As I re-entered Queens Park, Craig and Briony were there to meet me. As Briony joined me to walk up the steep incline, the comical juxtaposition of her pregnant state and my exhausted Ironman body meant it was hard to tell who was holding who back as we slowly paced up the hill. She filled me in on the traffic chaos that the Ironman event had brought to Bolton, turning the usually serene Sunday drive into a logistical nightmare. Most importantly she was absolutely fine, had managed to rest up and was here to support me, in one piece and in good spirits.

I inquired about Max and whether or not she knew how he was getting on, knowing she had planned to track both of us via the Ironman app and give him a cheer if he passed. I was half expecting him to be miles ahead at this time; although we'd never discussed our likely finishing times, I'd tracked his progress and his training times and had been really impressed. I thought I may see him, given that a four-lap marathon course led to lots of opportunities to catch glimpses of people much further along their journey.

226

To my surprise, I learned he was just a bit ahead of me, having only passed by a few minutes ago. This information sparked a new objective in my mind – to catch up with Max. As much as he would admit we were brothers on this challenge together, we both knew how super competitive we were! Energised by this goal, I increased my pace and soon spotted his unmistakable tall figure in the distance. I caught up and we exchanged quick updates of our days. Max had been, unsurprisingly, lightning fast in the water, getting out of the Pennington Flash in 1 hour 16 minutes. He'd flown through both transitions in nine minutes apiece (lessons to be learned here Chris!) but he had struggled like most of us on that punishing bike route. We acknowledged our shared experiences of the gruelling bike leg and the relief of being on the final discipline.

After parting ways with Max, I continued down Chorley Road. The atmosphere was noticeably livelier, the sky clearer, and with the pubs flanking the streets full of enthusiastic spectators. The cheers and slightly slurred shouts from the patrons added a party-like air to the event. As the evening progressed, the crowd's energy became more palpable, their encouragement fuelling my steps.

Navigating through Queens Park again, the area had transformed into a vibrant centre of activity. With the convergence of the final cyclists now on the course following the passing of the bike cut-off, and the faster runners who were finishing their last lap, the race was at its peak for competitors. The result meant the park was alive – crammed with supporters, music and a sense of excitement. As before, the end of the lap brought with it a new wristband, this time blue. It was a colourful testament to my progress and another milestone hit, and a reminder of the journey still ahead.

With two laps down and two to go, I felt a renewed sense of determination. The prospect of crossing the finish line, which so often during the training and even during my low points of the day itself seemed an impossible feat, was now within reach. Others may have been in a different frame of mind at this point, a dark place of suffering, and it would certainly make for a better narrative if I had been. For me though, the cheers of the crowd, the camaraderie of my fellow athletes and the unwavering support of my loved ones were propelling me forward and keeping the dreaded 'wall' at bay. In that moment I felt genuine and heartfelt joy. My body may well be knackered but I was more than just a participant in the Ironman; I was part of a community, a collective of individuals bound by a shared pursuit of extraordinary goals. This day had really brought the best of people to the surface.

As I commenced the third lap of the marathon, the light just starting to fade, a wave of elation washed over me. As I ran the maths, I realised that I was on the cusp of becoming an Ironman. Factoring in the remaining miles vs the allotted hours meant, by my foggy-minded calculations, that barring any unforeseen calamities I would now make it. The knowledge that I could technically walk the rest of the course and still earn the coveted title of an Ironman was incredibly liberating. It meant for the rest of the race I could really afford to enjoy the moment.

Yet, the knowledge that the finish was within reach seemed to have the complete opposite effect. Now, instead of slowing down, the unburdening of time pressure seemed to ignite a spark within me. To my own amazement, I found myself picking up the pace, clocking mile 18 in an impressive 8 minutes and 33 seconds. As my Garmin bleeped this alert, I stared at it in amazement – an unexpected triumph.

The support of Craig and Briony was instrumental during these crucial moments. Each time I passed them, their words of encouragement and cheers provided the much-needed motivation to push forward and they were a real reminder of how important people can be in your life.

As I collected my red band and exited the park for the final lap, I bid farewell to Craig and Briony, who told me they now planned to make their way to the finish line to await my arrival. Knowing they would be there and I should soon be with them filled me with an indescribable rush of excitement. The prospect of seeing their faces as I crossed the line propelled me forward with a new-found energy.

The streets of Bolton, once a daunting challenge, now felt like familiar friends. Each aid station was filled with the same familiar faces, every pub cheer was on repeat, and the gang of volunteers holding out the next-lap bands had become a frequent and welcome sight.

Embarking on the fourth and final lap, a sense of victory already bubbled within me. This felt like this should now be a celebratory victory lap, a culmination of relentless training, unyielding perseverance and a dream that was on the brink of becoming a reality. Pre-race I had had no idea how I would be feeling both physically and mentally at this point, but in that moment I decided this hour (or so) would be a chance to savour every moment of Bolton Ironman.

However, moments later as I slowly walked through the town centre, I was brought down to earth by the one man who had been my voice of reason throughout this journey. Coach Garrie's voice cut through the air, jolting me back to focus. 'This isn't an aid station, Chris, and it's not a bloody sponsored walk. Get running!' His reminder echoed our pre-race strategy, snapping me back into the athlete's mindset. It wasn't time to count my chickens just yet; it was time to put my foot down for one final push!

As I approached the next aid station, the euphoria of the last lap began to wane, and so did my adherence to the planned race nutrition strategy. Cravings took over, and I sought out everything the next few aid stations had to offer. Sorry gut, my taste buds had spoken! Helping myself to flat cola and salty crisps – a heavenly respite from the monotonous regime of gels and water – the thoughts of dodgy stomachs were trumped by the desires of my body. The change was invigorating, providing a much-needed boost for the final stretch.

It was during this lap that I encountered fellow athletes from the triathlon weekend, their faces lit up with joy and triumph. The vast majority were coming back into town at the end of their final laps. Their energy was infectious, and it was inspiring to witness their accomplishment as they sprinted towards their finishing line, radiating a freshness that belied the gruelling journey they had undertaken.

As I made what would be my final turn and headed back down Chorley Road, I encountered a true Ironman legend, the author of *Secrets of the Ironmen*, the one and only Iron Rookie. His book had been a guiding light in my own journey, and it was surreal to share a moment with him. I told him how inspiring he had been to me, and I thanked him as we jogged together. His words of encouragement to me, 'You're looking strong, crack on and get to that line,' filled me with a renewed sense of purpose and pride. Here was a guy I had read about and held on a pedestal. I was a lap ahead and he was telling me I was looking strong!

Pressing on, I secured my final band, this time yellow, a tangible symbol of my progress. The complete set were my ticket to the finishing chute as I began my descent into town. The anticipation was palpable as I knew this was my moment – Briony, a finishing line and the medal awaited me.

Chapter 45
Crossing the Threshold

The final stretch of Bolton's marathon route unfolded before me, marking the last leg of an epic journey and a tortuous but amazing day. As I slowly but surely came around the final bend towards the finish line, the grin on my face was there for all to see. Each step on the Ironman's red carpet was a culmination of countless hours of training, emotional highs and lows, and an unwavering commitment that had tested every fibre of my being over eight long months. The tune of 'Chelsea Dagger' by The Fratellis reverberated through the air, adding an electrifying energy to my final strides, 'Chelsea, Chelsea I believe …' booming away.

The sight of Briony and Craig among the cheering crowd was a heart-warming reminder of the support and love that had fuelled my journey. Their shouts and cheers propelled me into the finishing chute, and I found myself sprinting with a vigour I hadn't known I had left in me. I forgot all the pain of the last few hours and charged to the finishing line. My arms swung high, my feet pounded the carpet and I absorbed the infectious energy from the crowd, urging me on with every step.

The moment the announcer's voice boomed, 'Chris, you are an Ironman!' a surge of emotion overwhelmed me. I had read about this moment, watched other people going through it on YouTube and thought about this so often over the last few months. I had crossed the finish line with a marathon time of 4 hours 26 minutes and 6 seconds. That meant I clocked a total Ironman time of 14 hours, 23 minutes and 44 seconds – a time that wouldn't mean I would be qualifying for the Ironman World Championships anytime soon, but that was still comfortably under the much-feared cut-off. The realisation hit me – I was officially an Ironman!

As I slowed to a stop, a volunteer draped the Ironman medal around my neck. Its weight was a tangible reminder of the journey, each ounce representing a story of perseverance and dedication. I stared at the medal, admiring its intricate design – a majestic lion, its gaze embodying resilience and determination. It was a fitting emblem for an event that demanded nothing less than everything I had to give.

In that moment, a mixture of relief, pride and sheer joy washed over me. The trials of training, the early mornings, the late nights, the doubts and the triumphs – they had all led to this incredible achievement. This journey, this up and down roller coaster to becoming an Ironman: it was more than just a physical challenge; it was a transformative experience that reshaped not just my body, but my mind and spirit.

I stood there and soaked in the euphoria of the moment, the cheers of the crowd and the proud faces of Briony and Craig. A volunteer saved me bending down and removed the timing chip from my ankle. This was a day that would forever be etched in my memory; a day when I proved to myself that with determination, grit and a bit of humour, anything is possible. The journey to the Ironman finish line was a testament to the human spirit's capacity to overcome, endure and ultimately triumph.

As I staggered out of the Ironman exit, the scene was markedly different from the all-you-can-eat pizza and palpable camaraderie of yesteryears. The buffet of recovery snacks, finishers' shirts and masseuses that were normally on offer were notably absent, a stark reminder of the Covid restrictions still nipping at our heels. Instead of allowing us to linger in the post-race glow, volunteers swiftly directed us to the exit – no dawdling allowed.

I emerged from the tent, dazed but triumphant, into the waiting arms of my personal cheer squad. Craig and Briony enveloped me in an embrace, a nonverbal exchange that spoke volumes of the day's trials and triumphs. Briony was practically vibrating with energy, regaling me with tales of the day, the people she had encountered and the mini-adventures that had unfolded on the sidelines.

One man who was noticeably absent was Coach Garrie, ever the Ironman sentinel, his unwavering commitment meant he remained out on the course, a beacon of motivation for his athletes, vowing to stay until the very last of his collective had crossed the finish line. Our catch-up would have to wait.

And then there was Max – my unexpected ally, my brother-in-arms throughout this journey. I navigated through the dissipating crowd towards the finish line just in time to see him approach, his own victory within his grasp. I added my voice to the chorus of cheers as he crossed the line, a mere 23 minutes behind me. It was a moment of pure elation; he was grinning from ear to ear as he raced over the line and the announcer boomed 'Max, you are an Ironman'. I left him to his family; we'd catch up later, but now was his moment to share with his loved ones. Ironman may have altered its finish-line festivities, but the essence of the achievement – the personal battles won, the friendships forged and the self-discovery endured – remained untouched.

Operation Clean-Up was now the final piece of admin for the day and the lingering adrenaline was a welcome ally as we trekked to reclaim my gear. The ten-minute walk to gather my transition bags and my loyal Boardman, which had ferried me through 112 miles of tempestuous weather and emotional peaks, gave us time to reflect. As we approached the car park, my body, which had been pushed to its limits, protested at the sight of the stairs – a humorous, albeit slightly painful, end to an epic day. Craig, in his unwavering supportive role, effortlessly hoisted the bike into the vehicle. It always makes sense to make friends with a tree surgeon when anything needs hauling effortlessly around! His strength was a stark contrast to my current state of fatigue-encased elation.

The drive back to Manchester was accompanied by the sun's descent, casting golden hues over Bolton – a fitting tribute to the end of an arduous but triumphant journey. The car became a cocoon of contented silence, each of us lost in our thoughts and the shared experience of the day.

Arriving home, Briony whipped up a feast while I took the opportunity to wash away the grime of the race – but not the glory. A hot shower never felt so good, even if I had a few more tender areas after more than 14 hours of non-stop movement. I finally had the chance to ditch the clothes of the day and put on a fresh set, but I returned the Ironman medal to my neck as I went back downstairs to celebrate with my greatest allies.

The WhatsApp group was a flurry of activity, each message a story, a shared experience, a laugh, or a sigh of relief as tales of the day flooded in. We collapsed on to the sofa, our collective exhaustion manifesting in the comfortable silence between us. I sipped on a celebratory glass of red wine, but when I was not even half a glass down, I could feel my eyes drooping. The red liquid was a toast to the journey, to the support and to the unspoken understanding that what we had all achieved today was something extraordinary, but right now all I was good for was bed.

And so, I drifted off to sleep, my body clean but still enveloped in the afterglow of the day's events, my grip on the medal loosening but its presence a reassuring weight in my palm. It was the perfect end to an Ironman's day – worn out, washed clean and holding on to a tangible reminder that the impossible had been made possible.

As I sit down to pen the final lines of this journey, I can't help but marvel at how it spiralled from a haunting nightmare into a dream realised. Lying in that hospital bed, gasping for air and feeling the prick of IVs, I never imagined this journey would culminate in such a fulfilling triumph.

Back in 2019, had I managed to claw my way to the start line, or even stagger across the finish, the journey might have felt slightly barren, devoid of the rich tapestry of experiences I've since woven. The pneumonia, as brutal as it was, became an unexpected catalyst, propelling me into a voyage that extended far beyond the physical challenges of the Ironman. It forced me to accept my weaknesses, seek understanding and education from others, allowing myself to be vulnerable and accept the wisdom found in numbers.

Reflecting on the mosaic of faces that have become part of this narrative, I'm overwhelmed with gratitude. Coach Garrie, with his gruff wisdom and unwavering support; the eclectic band of fellow athletes from the WhatsApp groups and training weekends, each with their own story of grit; the camaraderie on those winding bike paths; and, of course, Max – my unexpected ally in this endurance test of life. These characters enriched the tapestry of my experience, infusing it with colour and depth.

But it was sharing this entire experience with Briony – and also Craig – that truly anchored my soul to the essence of this journey. From the gruelling training days to the exuberant shouts of encouragement as I rounded those final turns, their presence wove love and support into the very fabric of my Ironman story.

As I close this chapter, my Ironman medal no longer hangs around my neck, but is proudly mounted on the wall, not just as a badge of personal achievement, but as a beacon of collective effort and a reminder to always push myself, to learn more and to enjoy the ride, however bumpy. It reminds me that even the most solitary paths are brightened by the people we meet along the way, and that every finish line is a celebration of shared humanity.

This journey has taught me that the true richness of such an endeavour lies not in the solitude of the struggle but in the shared heartbeat of those who join you along the way. It's in the laughter, the shared pain, the stories exchanged over carb-loaded dinners and the quiet, understanding looks that say, 'We did this together.'

And as I move forward, with the memories of this journey etched into every fibre of my being, I know that I'm forever changed – not just by the Ironman itself, but by the spirit of unity it has instilled in me. For it's in the unity of our struggles and the sharing of our victories that we truly find strength, and it's this strength that will fuel my next adventure, whatever it may be.

Part 5: Epilogue

Chapter 46

The Next Finish Line – Family, Fatherhood and Finding Balance

The days that followed the Ironman truly felt like the calm after the storm. The next morning, we waved goodbye to Craig as he dashed back to Yorkshire early to get to work. Briony and I made a brief pilgrimage back to the now-quiet streets of Bolton. There, amidst the dismantling of transition areas and discarded large cardboard messages to loved ones, I returned to the official Ironman store to a add a permanent inscription to my Ironman medal, and, yielding to that sweet victory high, I finally indulged in some Ironman-branded gear, the merchandise I dared not touch before the race. The hoodies, caps and bags were all mine, ready to help me on my new mission, to tell every person I met that I had completed an Ironman!

Later that day we set off for Cornwall, where the rainy hills of Lancashire felt a world away, as we were promised a week of sun-soaked weather to match my adrenaline-soaked spirits. Cornwall greeted us with the promise of tranquillity, and Briony, ever the architect of joy, surprised me with a rented hot tub in her family's garden to help the limbs recover!

The week unfolded like a series of snapshots – vivid, joyful and decadently lazy. After eight months of almost daily training towards this one goal, it had unsurprisingly created an obsession, but an obsession with a goal that had a high degree of doubt over whether it would be realised. To have completed my goal meant that week was infused with that ease of life that only seems to come from the satisfaction of hitting a coveted milestone. Lounging under the Cornish sun in a hot tub, trading the taste of saltwater for the sweet drip of melting ice cream, the meals were no longer fuel for the gruelling miles ahead but a celebration of flavours, each bite a small rebellion against the regimented diet of a triathlete in training.

Briony and I filled the days with long walks on the beach, no longer on tight deadlines for the next turbo trainer session, or prepping training gear for the next day. It was in these moments, suspended between the effort and the ease, that I replayed the race in my mind, not with the scrutiny of a strategist but with the fondness of a storyteller.

The glory wasn't just in the medal or the title, it was in this aftermath – the freedom to just be, to live without the looming shadow of the next training session, the next early start, the next physical trial. Here, in this Cornish retreat, I found a peace that was as victorious as any finish line I had ever crossed.

As the days in Cornwall stretched out before us, the world beyond our sunny enclave felt a million miles away. Yet, my connection to that world, the one forged through shared suffering and triumph, remained alive through the chattering digital lifeline of our Ironman WhatsApp group. It buzzed with the after-stories – the good and the bad. If this had been a Hollywood movie, everyone's stories would have had fairy-tale endings, of smashed PBs and triumphs against the odds. However, this was Ironman, and it can be a cruel mistress in the real world. For some, the dream was snatched away by a puncture or technical issues. Others just simply couldn't beat the ticking time bomb of the dreaded cut-offs. Ironman it seemed was as much about the heartbreak as it was about the glory.

It was a sobering reminder of how downright tough and unfair this race could be. Some simply removed themselves from the group, Coach Garrie filling in the blanks. One guy uploaded a long video; while explaining he didn't make the bike cut-off in the conditions, he used the moment to share his gratitude for the group, for the humour and the love of the journey. He spoke not of defeat, but of deferred victory – there was talk of next time, of redemption, of battles yet to be won. I loved the fact, several months later, he went again and completed his Ironman journey with the finish he wanted.

As the week waned, the call came from Coach Garrie – a debrief that felt more like a fireside chat than a clinical analysis of times and performance. We dissected the day in detail, lingering on the highs and learning from the lows. Then, as the conversation drew to a close, he posed *the* question: 'Will I be coaching you for next year's Ironman?'

The question caught me amid the afterglow of accomplishment and with the tender beginnings of fatherhood on the horizon. Would I return to the crucible that forged this new version of myself – the one who saw dreams not as distant stars but as mountains to be scaled? I felt a twinge in my gut – the pull of the start line, to re-experience the pure enjoyment of the day itself, the amazing crowds, the allure of the journey, the possibility of going faster, pushing harder, doing better.

I asked for time to think, to weigh the desire against the practicalities of a life about to change with the arrival of our first child. Coach Garrie understood, of course. He knew better than anyone that the journey to Ironman is as personal as it is physical and that level of dedication is not an easy opt-in.

As I sat there, enveloped in the warmth of the hot tub, the pulsating water mirroring the still-tangible buzz of adrenaline from the race, I found myself momentarily ensnared by the seductive call of Ironman adventures in far-off lands. The promotional videos I began watching on YouTube, with their glossy sheen and epic soundtracks, were not just selling a race but a dream – a siren song for the endurance junkie in me. The three-minute race recaps attracted me to the cobblestoned streets of Copenhagen, the sun-drenched coastlines of Barcelona ... these weren't just locales, they were promises of another chance to dance with the dragon, to chase that finish-line feeling but in new, even more alluring settings (no offence to you Bolton!).

But then there was Briony. Throughout this journey, she had been the unseen force that kept me grounded, the steady hand on the tiller when the waters got rough. She had been there through every mile, every early morning, and every sacrifice, offering unwavering support and boundless encouragement. And now, as we stood on the cusp of a new chapter, her belly swelling with the promise of our future, the scales of my priorities shifted.

The look in her eyes said it all – it was a cocktail of pride, love and an unspoken plea for togetherness in the adventures that lay ahead. Adventures that wouldn't require a wetsuit or a bike, but would no doubt test us in ways Ironman never could. She didn't need to say it aloud but she did anyway! The message was clear. Our family, our team of two soon to be three, needed me more than the Ironman did. Ironman would be off the agenda for the foreseeable.

So, when the time came to give Coach Garrie my answer, it was with a profound sense of gratitude and finality that I declined. The journey to Ironman had been a transformative one, but it was time to apply the lessons learned to a different kind of endurance event – the marathon of fatherhood. My 'no' to next year's race wasn't just a response to a question, it was just confirmation of my commitment to the home team.

And so, as we packed our bags to leave the haven of our holiday retreat, I left behind any lingering what-ifs along with the ripples in the hot tub. I carried with me the strength I'd found on the course, ready to channel it into the shared journey ahead. Ironman had been a dream, but what awaited me was reality – and it was infinitely sweeter.

Ironman, for all its glory, is an insatiable beast, demanding every spare moment, every ounce of energy, and let's not even talk about the financial toll. It's a world where carbon fibre is king, and your social life – what's left of it – often revolves around training schedules and protein shakes. It's easy to get lost in the pursuit of personal triumphs, to be the main character in your own epic saga, where every pedal stroke and every stride is a verse in your Ironman ballad.

But there comes a time when the spotlight must shift and when the supporting cast steps forward, the narrative takes an unexpected turn. For me, that time came when our little Benjamin Finlay Sheard decided to make his grand entrance into our world. Born of hope, science and unwavering love, he arrived not with the fanfare of a finish line but with a gentle, life-affirming smile that outshone any medal I could ever earn.

His tiny hands, his infectious giggle, the way he zooms around with the reckless abandon of an innocent child who has not experienced those major falls (you wait until you get out on the Bolton cycle route, son). And just when we thought our hearts were full, along came Oliver Lucas Sheard almost two years to the day after Benjamin's arrival, doubling our joy and cementing our family's legacy. Our duo of IVF wonders, our living, breathing proof that the most extraordinary feats against the odds don't always require a race bib or a timing chip.

In their eyes, I see the reflection of the man Ironman helped me become – a man ready to embrace the ultimate endurance event: fatherhood. They are my new finish line, my better-than-best time, my podium. The race that began with a starter's gun in Bolton now continues at home, paced by baby giggles and peppered with nappy changes and nursery rhymes.

The Ironman journey was transformative, but this … this is transcendent. It's a testament to life's beautiful ability to evolve, to trade in the solitude of long-distance training for the chaos and camaraderie of family life. And as I watch

Benjamin and Oliver grow, each milestone a testament to love's enduring strength, I realise that the greatest adventures still lie ahead. They are my heart, my joy and the ultimate champions in the Sheard family Ironman legacy.

Nonetheless, the Ironman has reset my expectations, physically. In the quiet hush of pre-dawn light, my running trainers still find their rhythm on the pavement, a solitary figure tracing the familiar routes where once I trained with a singular focus. Early morning training, and finding room for the 17-hour training weeks alongside full-time work could be argued as the perfect precursor for fatherhood. And now, these runs are my sanctuary, a space to gather my thoughts before the delightful chaos of the day with Benjamin and Oliver begins. There's something about the solitude of these runs that brings clarity, a peacefulness that only the early morning can offer.

Briony, ever the gracious partner in my athletic pursuits, agreed to a new arrangement. The iron-clad Ironman training schedule was shelved, whole weekends couldn't be replaced by long swims and cycle rides. Bath time needed two sets of hands, and one of them could not be locked on a turbo trainer.

But that competitive desire still remained, determined not to retire to a more dormant life, with dad bods and being out of breath while chasing the kids in the park. The early morning runs continued; a few midweek early morning runs started to become that little bit faster. As I started to become a little more competitive, the running buggies were purchased, and the Sunday morning crack of dawn run became that little bit longer week by week.

Ironmans were off the agenda, I had agreed to that. But a new obsession began to creep in: the World Marathon Majors, six marathons across cities across the world – London, Berlin, Chicago, Boston, New York and Tokyo. I negotiated this in my mind: family trips – surely that's a tick? Marathon training must be more manageable – that's got to be a tick? Surely this would get Briony's approval … right?!

Chapter 47

The Thank-Yous

Where to begin. Recently Max and I, after the excitement of the news that this book was not only in the works, but had found someone mad enough to potentially publish it, dissected the journey we had completed two years previous. The biggest thing we realised, looking back, is how un-ashamedly selfish the Ironman can become. It absorbs not just your pound notes, but your time, your moods, it becomes your number one obsession. The impact of that could be far-reaching. You ask others to make sacrifices, whether it be work colleagues, life partners or friends. You ask people to sacrifice their weekends, all in a selfish pursuit that, come race day, is seen as all yours.

There is no way to reset that balance in just a few short sentences but I will do my best. Firstly, Coach Garrie – without him I have no doubt my journey from hospital bed to Ironman starting line would have gone full circle, and without his strict hand to guide me, I'd have over – or under-cooked the effort. This man is a very humble guy, but his words of wisdom, shoulder to cry on and voice of reason helped guide me to that finish line.

Next up are the heroes I met along the way: chiefly Max, but fellow riders, the fellow athletes from the training weekends and people I chatted to at the side of Salford Quays. Not all of us were given the Hollywood ending we wanted this time in Ironman, but we were all part of each other's journey.

The nameless people – the people who turned up on the day to cheer us on, and make the day what it was. What would this race have been like if Covid had restricted the crowds? It would definitely have been a lonely endeavour. Then the hundreds of people who volunteered on the day:

those who offered positive words at the marathon aid stations or handed over a fresh water bottle in the beat of the rain on the bike course. I tried to thank every one of you, despite my mood or my energy levels. Please, it doesn't matter if you are competing in the Ironman World Championships or your local 5k, always thank these people; these days would be impossible without them. The final nameless hero was my mechanical legend who I have no doubt saved me from a DNF on the bike course. If you were that guy working at Trafford Park Evans Cycles that day, and you remember a guy with a broken bike and a desperate face – thank you. The ten minutes you gave when you could have, by rights, turned me away, potentially literally changed my life.

Last but by no means least is Briony. There are no words. When you wrote the next chapter, you reminded me of ways you showed your support that I had forgotten – ferrying water bottles and snacks to Cheshire roadsides. Your confidence never waned, you were the ultimate supporter, rock and partner for this journey. It's so important in life we pick a partner who has belief and supports our endeavours – and there is no doubt I have found mine.

I genuinely mean it when I say that if I had hacked my way somehow to the finish line of Ironman 2019, I would have the medal, potentially all the gear but I genuinely feel that my life would be so much poorer. Firstly, spending time in hospital, battling pneumonia was humbling, a stark reminder how precious life and fitness can be. But most crucially, while the end result would be the same, my journey would have been a starker, more lonely and unfulfilling experience. I wouldn't have met these amazing people, some that are etched in some of my happiest memories and some that have remained lifelong friends.

I will finish with the words of an African proverb, that sums it up much better than I ever could: If you want to go fast go alone. If you want to go far go together.

Chapter 48
Some Words From Briony

So here I am, Briony, having navigated the intricacies of being an 'Ironman Widow' – though truth be told, I lean more towards the title of the proud wife of an Ironman. It might lack the catchy ring, but it captures the essence of this incredible journey my husband Chris and I embarked upon, full of determination, resilience and an undying fighting spirit.

Our life together suddenly unfolded in chapters that were both profound and unexpected. Chris's Ironman journey became a shared roller-coaster ride, an extraordinary adventure we both embraced, though we might not have been entirely prepared for the twists and turns it brought.

After the setback of his first Ironman attempt, my role as Chris's support system took centre stage. I, the eternal optimist, embarked on the task of piecing together a broken man. It wasn't just about the physical recovery; the mental hurdles were the real challenge. Chris, my husband, my best friend and my team-mate, needed more than just faith in his physical strength; he needed unwavering support to rebuild his confidence.

In the lead-up to race day, optimism was very firmly my default setting. Chris often teases me about navigating life like a scene from *500 Days of Summer* – music playing, people dancing, birds singing. But amidst the uncertainties, the inclement forecast and the haunting memories of Chris's initial attempt, my belief in him never wavered. Perhaps it was the pregnancy hormones swirling within me, but there was an unshakeable certainty in my mind that Chris would successfully conquer this Ironman challenge.

Being part of Chris's training crew was an honour, a role I embraced with pride. I may not have held any formal Ironman training qualifications, but my contribution was unique. From Copenhagen's training runs to the Malta half-marathon, where Chris powered past me, each milestone marked a step closer to his mental and physical resurrection.

Some of my fondest memories are of myself, pregnant, running loops round Salford Quays, observing and feeding back on Chris's swim strokes. And later, when I was less mobile, plotting cycling routes in the Cheshire countryside where I could meet him for hydration and nutrition stops. I wanted to be a tangible part of this unique experience. It can be a somewhat selfish and self-indulgent journey for the competitor, but Chris and I, a solid partnership, made sure to make it as much a shared and enjoyable experience as possible.

When race day arrived, I found a sense of calm amidst the chaos of such a big event. Well, almost. There was that one pregnant dash into the trees just before the start, a minor hiccup in an otherwise poised day. The Ironman app became my virtual companion, helping me track Chris's progress during the cycling leg. Despite missing the bike-to-run transition due to traffic woes, I secured a prime spot in Queens Park, cheering him on twice each lap, whilst enjoying an ice cream or two in between!

In this Ironman spectacle, my cheers weren't reserved for Chris alone. Max, a stranger turned friend on the course, became part of the narrative. The atmosphere was electric, emotions ran high, and by the third run lap Max twigged who this crazy pregnant lady was who kept cheering him on. After a sweaty hug on the final lap, I shouted 'see you at the finish line' and hot-footed it across to catch Chris in time.

There it was. The infamous Ironman finish line chute. The sound was deafening, the crowds several deep. But we fought our way to a front-row view as 'Chelsea Dagger', blaring from the speakers, completed the scene. And then came the moment we had all been waiting for – the proclamation of triumph, the five words that turned our shared dream into a reality: 'Chris, you are an Ironman!'

Chapter 49

The Gear Chronicle

During the epic saga of my triathlon training, I feel I spent a small fortune to get me to the start of the Ironman. So, in case anyone has any questions on what to buy and potentially what to avoid, I have created a kit list, including not just what got me through on the day, but also some of the mistakes I made along the way.

The swim:

The wetsuit: First and foremost was the wetsuit, the Excalibur of my triathlon toolkit, a 2XU Men P1 Propel Open water Triathlon Wetsuit. Purchased by Briony, she confesses there wasn't too much logic behind her choice beyond the strong reviews and the special offers available.

Neoprene mittens and booties: These are oddities to the uninitiated but treasures to the cold-water swimmer. These were not fashion statements but necessities for training in waters that were less 'refreshing' and more 'did I just time-travel to the Ice Age?' Seriously, when the open-water swimming commences and the month hasn't yet hit May, you'll be thankful. Purchased from Decathlon so were budget-friendly too.

Neoprene cap: This headgear might have made me look like an extra in a low-budget sci-fi movie but it was invaluable in retaining what I liked to call my 'thinking heat'.

In the frigid waters of my training sessions, this cap was a lifesaver, literally keeping me from freezing out there. It even joined me on race day, worn discreetly under my official swim cap like a secret weapon against the cold.

Best buy:

Total Immersion Swimming course: My best purchase, however, was less about gear and more about skill. The Total Immersion Swimming course was a game-changer, a masterclass in the art of aquatic efficiency. A quick search for Total Immersion Swimming and Tim Ferris will sell it to you much better than I can.

Worst buy:

Bespoke goggles: Where there's light, there must be shadow, and in the world of Ironman swimming gear, my bespoke goggles were that shadow. Supposedly moulded for every contour of my face, so no water could ever penetrate them, I admit I fell for the hype and paid the premium. The reality was, this was an expensive mistake and, after a few frustrating sessions, they were confined to the drawer and I used an off-the-shelf pair. I'll avoid naming the company, but for me they were no better (actually worse) than off-the-shelf pairs.

The bike ride:

The Wahoo Kickr Turbo Trainer: Central to my indoor training kingdom was the Wahoo Kickr Turbo Trainer. This beast of machinery was the cornerstone of my cycling regime. No excuses when the training kicked in in earnest in deepest darkest winter, and the vital link to Coach Garrie's brutal training sessions.

The Wahoo Kickr Headwind Fan: Now this was a luxury – and one I would have resisted if it hadn't been another sterling present from Briony. The Wahoo Kickr Headwind Fan took the experience up a notch. It wasn't just a fan; it was an intelligent wind simulator, adjusting its gusts to match the intensity of my workout. This piece of equipment turned each ride into a more realistic road experience, minus the actual road. Plus, it kept the room chilled as I sweated away.

The Boardman SLR 8.9c Road Bike: My steed for the journey and a marvel of engineering that balanced performance with affordability. Its carbon frame was both light and sturdy, a perfect companion for the gruelling training and the eventual race day with the hills I was due to face. Plus, priced at £550 it was a steal (possibly literally) from eBay.

Cero evo alloy wheelset: The WhatsApp group's Gear Gurus did convince me on one minor tweak – an upgrade on the wheels. While a carbon wheel set was beyond my budget, I sprung for a pair of 1.5kg wheels, as, in the ever-desperate search for marginal gains, every weight drop was going to help.

The Garmin Edge 820: My navigator through this odyssey was the Garmin Edge 820 bike computer. This little device was like the mission control of my rides, providing me with real-time data on speed, distance and everything in between. For a stats-obsessed geek like me, it was crucial.

Zwift: My virtual training ground, a digital world where I could ride with athletes from around the globe. It turned each training session into an interactive experience, complete with competitions, challenges and the ever-important bragging rights.

Rouvy: However, the crown jewel of my cycling gear was Rouvy. This platform elevated my training with its realistic routes and races. It was like having the world's best cycling routes at my fingertips, each ride a new adventure, a new challenge to conquer.

Best Buy:

Bike Fit: The best investment in my cycling arsenal wasn't a piece of equipment but a service – the bike fit. This personalised fitting session was transformative, turning my Boardman from a mere bicycle into an extension of my body. Every adjustment, from the saddle height to the handlebar reach, was tailored to my physique and riding style, ensuring optimum comfort and efficiency. It was a revelation, reducing the risk of injury and elevating my riding experience. The difference pre and post bike fit was amazing and, even if the budget is tight, I'd recommend it. You'll spend the bulk of your day on the bike, and it's imperative you don't roll off it with aches and pains ahead of the run.

Worst Buy:

The Elite Aeton Aero Drinks System: Then came my less-than-stellar investment. Envisioned as a sleek, aerodynamic solution to my hydration needs, this drinks system instead became a fumbling, spill-inducing contraption. It made my bike top-heavy and, following the wise words of Coach Garrie, was ditched after its first real-life run out. Stick to your classic bottle and holder combos if you are not prepping for a flat course and are not riding a tri-specific bike.

The Run:

The Nike Vaporfly 4% running shoes: Leading the charge was this footwear equivalent of a Formula 1 car. These weren't just running shoes, they were a technological marvel, imbued with the promise of increased efficiency and speed. I probably wore them a little too frequently on the training runs and should have saved them for race day, but once my trainers arrived in a US-themed stars and stripes there was no way I would wear anything else for my own 4 July celebration.

Goodr running glasses: Cheap, affordable, I won't go overboard in terms on the sell on these ones. Goodr comes across as a very cool company, providing their glasses at a really affordable rate. Most importantly, they were just great running glasses that stayed on my head without any fuss and crucially they kept the sun out of the eyes, when it bothered to turn up!

Runderwear: The unsung hero of my running gear was the Runderwear. Comfort in running is often dictated by what you don't notice, and Runderwear was the epitome of this. Seamless, chafe-free and as supportive as a best friend, they were the foundation of my running comfort.

Compressport Anti-Blister Socks: Then there were these amazing socks. Blisters are the bane of long-distance runners' lives, but these socks were my shield against them. Each pair was a guardian for my feet, a blend of comfort and protection that kept the dreaded blisters at bay.

Best Buy:
Maurten gels: The crown jewel of my running gear, however, was the Maurten gels. These weren't just energy gels, they were a powerhouse of nutrition. In each sachet was a blend of carbohydrates and electrolytes, formulated to keep me going when my energy reserves started to flag. They were like rocket fuel, propelling me forward when my legs screamed for respite.

Worst Buy:
Caffeine gummies: On the flip side, my foray into caffeine gummies was less successful. Designed as an energy booster, they instead became a test of my digestive fortitude. Each chew was a gamble, a Russian roulette of whether it would provide a burst of energy or a bout of stomach cramps. They taught me a valuable lesson – sometimes the old ways (or gels, in this case) are the best.

Special Mention: TrainingPeaks
This became the digital bridge between Coach Garrie and I. Once he had uploaded my sessions to complete for the week ahead, I would then access them via the TrainingPeaks platforms. Connecting direct to my Garmin watch or bike computer, my completed sessions would automatically sync

with the platform for assessment. Worth the premium and took the heavy lifting out of passing feedback manually between us.

I hope this list provides some useful information. Remember, this is purely put together from my own experience, so you should always try things out as part of your training. In the now famous words of Coach Garrie, three weeks out from the Ironman, the term 'new' is a banned word! Stick to this mentality and you'll avoid last-minute rogue and expensive purchases as the race nerves kick in.

Good luck out there!